SACRED SYMBOLS

SACRED
SYMBOLS

CLARE GIBSON

BARNES
&NOBLE
BOOKS
NEW YORK

Published by Saraband Inc., PO Box 0032, Rowayton, CT 06853-0032, USA.

1998 Barnes and Noble

Copyright © 1998 Saraband Inc.
Design © Ziga Design
Editor: Robin Langley Sommer
Art director: Charles J. Ziga
Graphic designer: Wendy Ciaccia
Photo editors: Sara Hunt, Nicola Gillies

ISBN: 1-887354-18-2

Printed in China

10 9 8 7 6 5 4 3 2 1

Left: *An expressive Madonna and Child from the early Renaissance.*

page 2: *Clockwise from top left: cave painting of a horse from Lascaux, France; mosaic of St. Joseph from a Greek church; Anubis, jackal-headed god of embalming, from an Egyptian Book of the Dead; the compassionate Buddha in the state of Nirvana, from the Far East.*

Contents

Introduction

La nature est un temple où de vivants piliers
Laissent parfois sortir de confuses paroles;
L'homme y passe à travers des forêts de symboles
Qui l'observent avec des regards familiers.

Nature is a temple where, from living pillars,
Confused words are sometimes allowed to escape;
Here man passes, through forests of symbols,
Which watch him with looks of recognition.

—CHARLES BAUDELAIRE (1821–67),
LES FLEURS DU MAL (1857) "Correspondances," no. 4.

S acred concepts are inextricably linked with the symbols that express them. Indeed, humankind's earliest religious activities were first learned about through the symbolic images of the sacred that are represented in the rock paintings that adorn such late Paleolithic cave systems as those of Lascaux, France, and Altamira, Spain. Their hunting scenes, which feature large herds of game animals, can be regarded as a graphic form of wish-fulfillment, while the abstract, geometric forms that they contain are thought to express cosmic beliefs. Today, the world rejoices in a wealth of sacred and religious beliefs, all of which have their own richly symbolic vocabularies. But how did humankind develop such a sophisticated sense of the sacred, and what is the function of sacred symbols?

Opposite: Sacred concepts may be expressed through symbolic architectural devices; the pyramidal form of this Buddhist shrine in Nepal represents the stages of ascent toward spiritual enlightenment.

Left: The symbolic images in this Native American Klamath rock painting from northern California are remarkably similar to those seen in the cave art of other continents.

DEVELOPMENT OF COSMOLOGIES AND SACRED BELIEFS

Ancient forms of symbolic expression like those seen in late Paleolithic cave art reflect the need of early humans to make sense of a world whose natural forces, on which their survival depended, seemed to behave in a frighteningly unpredictable fashion. Our earliest ancestors lacked even the most rudimentary scientific knowledge and therefore regarded the workings of nature with understandable awe. What did they perceive as the cause of such natural phenomena as the rising and setting of the sun and moon and the course of the seasons, upon whose regular cycles they depended so completely? Demonstrating humankind's enduring need to rationalize and to attempt to control, they quite logically ascribed the forces of nature to supernatural powers, thus personifying such otherwise inexplicable phenomena as the sun, moon, wind and rain as mighty gods who

had to be appeased if their favors were to continue. It was believed that failure to do so would result in the gods' displeasure manifested in the form of disastrous punishments—drought, flooding or famine.

Thus developed the first cosmogonies and cosmologies—the theories regarding the creation of the natural world and the gods who ruled it—and this ancient belief in supernatural beings who ruled the universe and determined human fate laid the foundation for the world's subsequent multitude of faiths. The rationale behind the earliest religions concentrated inevitably on the need to sustain life. Therefore, ensuring the continuation of natural fertility was of overriding importance.

With the development of agricultural systems over the ages, people gained some measure of control over their environment. Thus regulation of the natural world by ritual became less central to sacred beliefs, giving way to humankind's ever-increasing desire for spiritual fulfillment. The rites and rituals of animism, totemism, lunar and solar religious cultures through polytheism, monotheism, pantheism and the moral philosophical thought of more recent centuries, demonstrate an increasingly abstract, but not necessarily superior, view of the sacred. All these types of belief continue to be practiced today; some of the most ancient have even enjoyed a New Age revival.

THE EVOLUTION OF SACRED SYMBOLS

Because sacred thought involves the intangible and supernatural, it cannot help but be expressed symbolically. The primary function of a symbol is to express a concept by employing a means of visual shorthand. A symbol has many advantages over the written or spoken word: it transcends the barriers of language; its message can be instantly registered and absorbed; and, most importantly in terms of the sacred, it

Above: A symbol-filled scene from the Egyptian Book of the Dead, depicting Re (center) and other deities riding in his solar boat.

Background: The sun and moon, the first dominant symbols of the sacred.

Opposite, top: A detail from the cave art of Lascaux, in France, representing the bison on which the artist's tribe depended for sustenance.

Opposite, bottom: An intricate depiction of an elephant graces this rock face in the eastern Sahara region of Africa, once a verdant area.

encourages a mystical or metaphysical reaction in achieving a closer communion with the sacred. Symbols are powerful and complex forms of communication despite their graphic simplicity.

Sacred symbols are so closely associated with the religious concepts they represent that it might be pertinent to ask which came first, the religion or the symbol? The sun, for example, became a symbol of the omnipotent sun god of many religions, yet it was the sun itself that was the focus of worship for the followers of solar religions. It was natural for early humans to think in terms of analogy and logical for them to compare the relationships of their supernatural gods with their own. Thus the sun, clearly the dominant object in the sky because of the warmth and light that it gives, was associated with an all-powerful masculine figure—the fiery epitome of strength,

Below: An ancient Egyptian ritual involving the votive offering of geese and hens—both birds were associated with mother goddesses, and hence symbolized natural fertility.

passion and virility. The moon, by contrast, was regarded as the sun god's passive female consort. Through her ability to regulate the lunar cycle that influences the ebb and flow of the tides, the queen of heaven became the patroness of fertility. Although both sun and moon were supremely important in early religions, the archaeological discovery of numerous earth-mother figures has shown that ancient humans initially revered the lunar goddess, the provider of fertility, over the solar god, to whom her pre-eminent position was later subordinated.

The sun and the moon were the most important early sacred symbols, supernaturally linked yet standing in opposition to one another. As the dominant symbols of the sacred, they lent their respective characteristics to the elements of the natural world that surrounded early humankind: thus birds like the eagle were regarded as

solar creatures and depicted as living in perpetual conflict with the primary representatives of the lunar principle, most notably the serpent or dragon. Indeed, most religious belief is founded on the concepts of duality and contrast, in which the characteristics of each god have their counterparts in those of another. Some, more "perfect," gods or supernatural forces inherently reconcile such conflicting features, and this principle of harmony is best illustrated in Taoist thought, where perfection can be achieved only when the opposing forces of yin and yang are in complete balance. Although generalization begs the exception to the rule, over the millennia a widely known set of antithetical symbolic principles evolved, some of whose elements can be simplified as follows: masculine/feminine, lunar/solar, active/passive, light/darkness, heat/cold, heaven/earth, good/evil, natural/un-natural and life/death.

As their cave art demonstrates, early humans quickly grasped the inherent potential of the symbol both to express sacred beliefs pictorially and to conjure up deities, the magical transformation of the symbol being effected in the human imagination. Gods in particular can be symbolized in either iconic form, in which their physical appearance is depicted, or in aniconic form, in which there is no visual resemblance to the deity (as in the

Above: When spun, Buddhist prayer wheels are believed to send the printed prayers contained within them flying toward the heavens.

Below: The hybrid forms of these Thai temple guardians symbolize protection against the desecration of the sacred.

Right: Sacred concepts and symbolism are inseparably intertwined, as seen in this classical image of Spring bearing flowers. Humanity has consistently expressed elements of faith through symbolic representation.

Christian Holy Trinity, for example). Sacred symbols need not assume pictorial forms alone: religious architecture, oral chants and mantras, or objects like the Christian rosary are all imbued with symbolic resonance to those who believe in their transcendental power.

In addition to representing and revealing sacred concepts, the symbol also acquired additional functions. While such archetypes as the sun are universally recognized, the inherent power of other symbols lay in their ability to conceal: the mysterious hieroglyphics whose meaning was known only to the ancient Egyptian priesthood, for example; the secret symbols of the Greco-Roman mystery religions; or the fish that early Christians used as a more subtle form of religious identification than the cross to elude Roman persecution.

It must be stressed, however, that a sacred symbol's primary power lies in its significance to the believer. If a symbol becomes too well known, or is used in the wrong context, its original sacred meaning can be destroyed. Take, for example, the Nazis' degradation of the swastika from one of the world's most ancient and universal symbols of regeneration and movement into one of dictatorship and destruction. Less ominous is the example of the pearl, once sacred to the lunar goddess, and now valued primarily for its monetary worth as jewelry.

ARCHETYPAL AND UNIVERSAL SACRED SYMBOLS

The similarity of many of the symbols represesenting the beliefs of the world's various faiths — however disparate their origins in terms of both geography and time — as well as their principles of opposition, is remarkable. Most thunder or sky gods, for example, such as the Norse Thor or the Greek Zeus, are represented by a thunderbolt, which often takes the form of an ax.

This correspondence could, of course, be mere coincidence, or may be explained by syncretism — the fusion of the deities of one culture with those of another, just as the Romans adapted the characteristics of the ancient Greek gods to suit their purposes. However, the psychologist Carl Gustav Jung (1875–1961) had a different explanation for these extraordinary similarities, one that he believed lay buried deep within the human psyche. "It was manifestly not a question of inherited ideas, but of an inborn disposition to produce parallel images, or rather of identical psychic structures common to all men, which I later called the archetypes of the collective unconsciousness," stated Jung in his work *Symbols of Transformation* (1956).

Jung's seminal studies of symbolism postulated his now widely accepted theories regarding both the existence of the human collective unconscious and the universal archetypes that it contains. According to Jung, inherent in the individual human psyche is an ancient collective memory, in which humankind's universal experience is symbolized by means of the archetypes, or primordial symbols, such as the earth mother, or the sun and the moon. Since the archetypes of the collective unconscious are common to us all, whatever creed or race, it is hardly surprising that these images should have been consciously selected to represent the many sacred concepts of the world's religions. And because these archetypal symbols are familiar to us all—on an unconscious as well as conscious level—we respond to them both intuitively and rationally.

PRIMORDIAL SACRED SYMBOLS

It is mainly as a result of Jung's pioneering work with symbolism that we now recognize that the "universal" symbols common to many world religions are archetypal products of humankind's "natural religious function," as Jung described it. Two of the most important universal symbolic images that Jung studied were the circle, or mandala—a symbol of eternity and unity—and the cosmic tree, which can be regarded both as a symbol of the self, or as a cosmic axis (axis mundi) linking the underworld, earth and heavens. Included among the many other universal sacred symbols are the dot, symbolizing the supreme being; the cosmic mountain, which signifies the creation of the world from the murky primeval waters; the egg or seed from which life springs; the square, representing the earth; the spiral, symbolizing cosmic force; and the wheel, signifying solar power. These, and many more, belong to a powerful symbolic language that communicates directly with our unconcious ability to recognize the sacred.

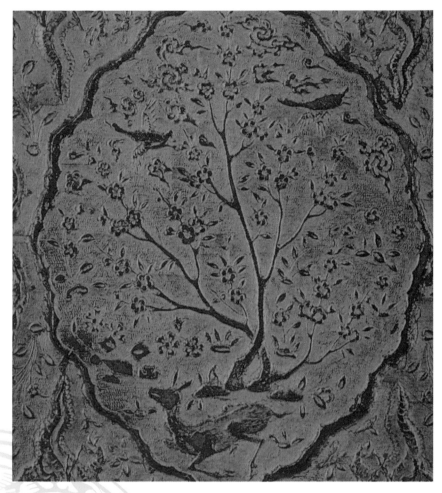

ABOUT THIS BOOK

Sacred symbols can be properly understood only within the context of the particular religion that endows them with their transcendental power. For this reason, the key tenets of each system of sacred belief contained in this book are briefly discussed in order to explain the significance of the faith's sacred symbolism to its adherents.

In the words of mythologist Joseph Campbell, "It has always been known [that] the prime functions of mythology and rite supply the symbols that move the human spirit forward." The symbols contained in this book cannot encompass all those that are regarded as sacred by the world's multitude of credos, but they include some of the most important and representative. Hopefully, they will not fail to educate, inspire and elevate.

Above: An exquisite Islamic tapestry representing the tree of life. The universal symbol of the tree has profound significance in most world cultures, and, among many other concepts, can represent the cosmic axis, life, knowledge and the individual self.

Background: An Islamic image of the wheel, a universal symbol of the cycle of life.

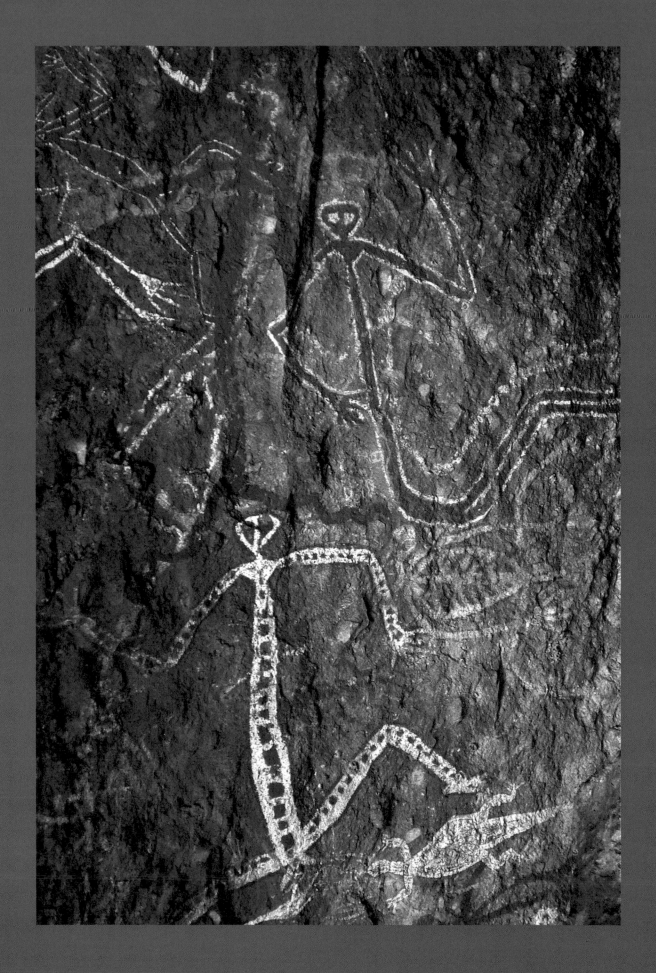

Shamanic & Tribal Sacred Symbols

Reflecting the supreme importance of, and reverence for, the natural environment, the symbols that primarily inform the beliefs and rituals of shamanic and tribal societies are those of nature. The sacred ties that bind tribal societies together are primarily totemic, asserting both the supernatural power attributed to both plant and animal life and their significance in determining the tribe's hierarchies of kinship and its beliefs. Totemism is common to African, Australian Aboriginal, Pacific, Native American and other tribal societies, which often share archetypal mythological symbols, including the culture hero, hero twins and trickster. Shamanic and tribal religions are among the most ancient: their strength is such that they have endured for millennia. However, the complex religions of Mesoamerica no longer exist as significant cultural forces, as they were exterminated by the Spanish conquistadors from the sixteenth century onward. This chapter discusses the symbols of these sacred beliefs, which, although dispersed throughout the world, demonstrate a remarkable similarity of tradition.

ELEMENTAL SYMBOLS OF THE SACRED

Shamanism emerged more than twenty thousand years ago in Central Asia and Siberia (whose Tungu word "*saman*" evolved into the generic name "shaman"). Today shamanism encompasses similar belief systems in other parts of the world, including those of the Native American tribes of the North American Plains, of Tierra del Fuego and of some Australian Aboriginal societies. However, it remains strongest among such Siberian peoples as the Tungus, Lapps and Inuits. Essentially comprising a mystical communion with spirits believed to exist in otherworldly zones of reality, shamanism is less a faith in which the whole community participates actively than one centering on the ability of the shaman himself (usually a man) to interact with supernatural forces on behalf of the tribe.

Although some of those who become shamans have inherited the role, most become aware of their mission through intense spiritual visions, which may occur through ritual seeking out or during the fevered dreams of an illness. Such visions provide the shaman's first contact with the spirit helpers who will assist and guide him throughout his life. Foremost among these helpers is a single, tutelary spirit, which could be that of a departed person strongly linked with the individual (an ancestor, or previous shaman, for example), or a totemic, animal-like spirit that acts as a guardian. However, many other spirits, all of

Opposite: Rock paintings, such as this Australian Aboriginal depiction of scenes drawn from the Dreaming, are the earliest forms of human artistic, sacred and symbolic expression.

Left: An Inuit shaman's mask dating from around 1900. Such masks symbolize the shaman's spirit helper, and their ferocious forms are intended to terrify his supernatural opponents.

Right: The insistent beat of the shaman's drum—traditionally decorated with symbols of the forces that he encounters in the spirit world—helps him to enter ecstatic trances.
Below: Dramatic features of the natural landscape, like these monumental rock formations in Utah, symbolize the sacred powers and concepts that still have resonance in tribal cultures.
Background: A conch shell, sign of a good journey.

which have specific characteristics or functions, also ally themselves with the shaman. Once identified, he will be trained by an experienced practitioner before undergoing a rite of initiation that involves his symbolic death, dismemberment and rebirth as a new, empowered mediator with the spirit world. In some shamanic cultures, particularly among Australian Aboriginals and Native Americans, the spirits may confer stones, shells, or crys-

tals on their protégés, which are then inserted under the skin as a symbol of endowment with magical powers of clairvoyance and healing. From now on, the shaman will live in two dimensions: that of earthly existence, and that of the transcendent realm. This consists of the heavens and the underworld, both of which are symbolically connected with, not separated from, the Earth by the cosmic tree.

As far as the members of the tribe are concerned, the shaman is responsible for ensuring their physical, mental and spiritual health, which are believed to be inseparable, but which may be adversely affected by the influence of malign or unsettled spirits (of plants, animals, geographical features such as mountains or rivers, or of the dead), or by the souls of the living that have become "lost." Through his unique function as an intermediary between the spiritual and physical worlds, the shaman is thus simultaneously the community's physician and seer. Not only does his benevolent influence extend to the world of the living, he also ensures that the spirits of departed human beings and animals are conducted safely to their proper realm, where they will find fulfillment and present no danger to the living through random wanderings. Thus the shaman's function is holistic, reflecting the primordial view that all the components of the universe are interconnected: he alone can travel the spheres of the cosmos to bring about a harmonious interaction between the spirits and humans beings.

In order to travel to otherworldly realms, the shaman must enter a deep, ecstatic trance, during which he remains fully in control and aware of events. Shamans

employ many methods for attaining this trancelike state, including fasting, meditation, or ingestion of hallucinogenic substances. The most common methods are dancing and chanting to the repetitive, hypnotic beat of a drum or rattle to free themselves from earthly restraints and travel into the spirit world. During this cosmic journey, the shaman may take flight by changing his shape, be assisted by spirit helpers in the form of such animals as horses, snakes, or birds, or make use of a supernatural vehicle like a "spirit boat." Whichever method he uses, he will seek out the spirit concerned—perhaps the wandering soul of one whose sickness has

been caused by its disembodiment. Once it is located, it must be reunited with its ailing physical body. Or his objective may be a hostile sorcerer against whom he must battle. The danger involved in making such journeys is never underestimated by the shaman, for failure may result in his madness, or even death. During these ecstatic trances, awed spectators may observe the shaman performing near-supernatural feats of strength and fortitude, hear him speaking in animallike or unknown tongues, or discern the presence of the spirits by such signs as the appearance of a rope in the sky or other inexplicable phenomena, including spontaneous combustion.

Should the illness of the patient whom the shaman seeks to heal remain uncured during the course of his trance, the shaman may still receive pertinent advice from his

Above: *During his out-of-body journeys to the spiritual realm, the shaman may seek assistance from the natural masters of the sky, of which the mighty eagle is perhaps the greatest.* **Left:** *The shaman's clothing itself is regarded as possessing magical powers or special significance: its decoration, like that of ritual artefacts, is designed to emphasize the shaman's identification with the spirit world.*

Right: In traditional belief, the strength and ferocity of the bear make it a formidable ally to the shaman in his desperate struggle against the powers of evil. Below: The ritual rattle, like this Tlingit example from about 1800, is a valuable part of the shaman's magical armory. Background: The stag, identified with virility and the Tree of Life. Opposite: Tribal cave paintings were a form of sacred wish-fulfillment, a plea for divine favor. The serpent is a powerful symbol in most tribal systems, often representing a culture hero. Background, the beetle signifies regeneration.

spirit helpers as to its cause. Soul "loss" is only one explanation for physical sickness. Another blames the insertion of a malignant object into the patient's body by an evil spirit or magician. If the shaman's helping spirits make this diagnosis, he may use a sucking pipe to draw out the disease-causing object, which the benevolent spirits will then absorb and neutralize. In addition to his role as a healer, the shaman may also interpret dreams, make prophecies and intercede for favorable weather, thus magically ensuring abundant plant and animal life upon which the community's livelihood is dependent.

Given the inextricable relationship between shamanism and the natural world, the most powerful shamanic symbols are those of nature. Such symbols may take the form of the cosmic tree, which links all those worlds to which the shaman alone has access, or of his closest spiritual helpers, who are often personified in the form of animals, including reindeer, jaguars, stags, coyotes or bears; such birds as the eagle; or plants like the hallucinogenic peyote. Antlers are especially important symbols, not only because they

resemble the branches of the cosmic tree, but because their zigzag form can represent a bridge to the spirit world and their height, a striving for spiritual wisdom; thus, they frequently adorn a shaman's cap.

These natural symbols are often used to decorate the shaman's tools and ritual garments, which are themselves highly symbolic artefacts. His sucking pipe, drum and rattle, the instruments that enable him to cure illnesses and enter a trancelike state, are potent symbols of magical power. The drum, whose monotonous beat represents the sound of creation, and which some believe is carved from the wood of the cosmic tree, can be equated with a "spirit boat," which carries the shaman to the spiritual realm. The rattle performs a similar function in evoking the spirits. The shaman's cloak, made of animal hide, often confirms his identification with his guardian spirit, as does his mask, which helps him to assume the characteristics of the creature portrayed and, if necessary, frightens away hostile spirits. Other symbolic instruments include the feathered arrow, signifying ascent to heaven, and the staff, which can both repel evil spirits and serve in the same manner as the magical wand of Western tradition.

AFRICAN TRIBAL SYMBOLS

There are hundreds of African tribes, each with its own sacred belief systems and rituals. Thus it is unwise to regard the continent's many faiths as melding into a single, conveniently homogeneous, religion. Bearing this caveat in mind, it is possible to generalize to some extent so as to identify certain features common to the majority of African tribes.

Many African sacred traditions, for example, teach that the world was created by a single supreme being, but unlike Christianity, Judaism, or Islam, tribal worship is not centered upon this rather remote deity, but on the lesser, more approachable divinities that personify one aspect of the supreme being, regulate a particular aspect of nature, or preside over a specific locality. As in so many tribal societies, animals and birds often serve as important totemic or cult creatures, who, in the dim mists of time, guided and instructed the first human beings in the ways of survival. The serpent, raven and spider, for instance, are all regarded as culture heroes by certain tribes, whose legends also attribute a trickster role to some creatures, like the spider and the hare. Other animals are considered sacred because of their symbolic qualities. For example, the speed of the antelope represents the elusiveness of the spirits. In most African societies, plant life assumes fertility symbolism: among the Dogon, the calabash (or gourd) is regarded as a solar-related symbol of fecundity; when cut in two it represents the realms of heaven and earth.

Then there are the ancestral spirits, which are believed to remain actively involved in the lives of their descendants, acting as intercessors between human beings and the supreme being. Linked to the individual or tribe by ties of blood, ancestral spirits are more tangible than other supernatural beings and are frequently addressed by

and Ibo, believe that ancestors are reincarnated in their descendants. This credo is particularly relevant in those tribes that are ruled by a divine king, whose power—often including that of rain-making and divination—is perpetuated through the repeated reincarnation of a divine hero, and whose subjects worship him by means of elaborate rites.

In supernatural terms, the majority of African tribal beliefs identify a clear struggle between the powers of good and evil, a battle in which the medicine man or witch doctor plays a vital role. The reason behind any misfortune that befalls an individual or tribe must first be ascertained. To do this, the witch doctor will either enter a mediumistic trance to seek the advice of ancestral or other spirits, consult an oracle such as the benge poison oracle of the Zande, or refer to the divine wisdom recorded in tribal myth, as in the Yoruba Ifa oracle. Either the displeasure of an ancestor or the malignant influence of a sorcerer will be revealed, while in some cases the possession of an individual by a spirit will be diagnosed and the spirit accordingly exorcised. Once identified, the problem must be resolved by means of the correct ritual.

Indeed, ritual enactment is crucial to African sacred belief and practices, representing the means whereby humans can actively influence the spirits. Ritual is inherently symbolic, and its effects are further reinforced by the use of symbolic costumes and artefacts. Specific

Above: An African witch doctor presides over a healing ritual in which chickens play a central role.
Right: An Ashanti figurine; such statuettes are created ritually to symbolize the spiritual essence of a tribal ancestor. ***Opposite, top:*** *The witch doctor's unique costume and mask enable him to assume the characteristics of the creature symbolized, in this case a fox.*
Opposite, below: *This symbolic mask from the Ivory Coast would be used during sacred rituals designed to elicit the support and protection of tribal divinities.*
Background: *An African ibex with crescent-shaped horns, which are sometimes used in rituals.*

prayer and sacrifice in the hope that they will wield their influence on behalf of their kin. The practice of ancestor veneration reflects the importance of the bonds of kinship within African tribal communities, as well as the respect that is accorded to elders. Indeed, few important decisions are made without first consulting the ancestral spirits, who are also regarded as the guardians of tribal custom and possessors of the power to punish those who displease them with famine, illness, or other calamitous misfortunes. After tribal elders die, provided that they are considered worthy of respect, they are elevated to ancestral status by means of various rites. Their continuing presence within the community is symbolized by the creation of an ancestral figure, usually in the form of a carved statuette, which is imbued with power by the appropriate rituals, and which some are convinced contains the individual's very life essence. Additionally, some African tribes, such as the Benin

rituals and ceremonies may be prescribed for rain-making; healing; rites of passage such as birth, marriage and death; consecration of ancestral spirits; and initiation into secret societies or adulthood. During the course of such rituals, the participants frequently don masks that symbolize the ancestral, totemic and other divine beings which have special significance to the tribe, protect the wearers and impart their unique, supernatural qualities to them, allowing the participants in the ritual to transcend their lowly human state. Participants may additionally be painted with symbolic marks, or may wear the appropriate costumes associated with the ritual. Both forms of decoration are regarded as being important means of harnessing the powers of the spirits thus signified. Following a set pattern as dictated by tribal myth, and frequently accompanied by chants and the insistent drumbeat that represents the echo of existence and induces an ecstatic trance, the ritual is re-enacted as both a symbol of the tribe's sacred beliefs and an affirmation of its desire for sympathetic treatment by the spirits.

As well as participating in collective rituals, many individuals hope to control their own destiny with the help of a personal power object or fetish—either a single artefact such as a talisman or amulet, or a bundle of symbolic objects or materials thought to possess supernatural power. These are used not only for protection but also for offensive purposes. Other objects, such as fertility dolls, are also powerful symbols of wish-fulfillment. Although they are not considered as effective as communal rites, or the magical ability embodied in the witch doctor, these personal items may be regarded as instruments which symbolically empower the individual, who is otherwise helpless when faced with the overwhelming powers of supernatural forces.

Below: The frenzied dancing of Voodoo devotees drives them into a trancelike state, thereby suppressing all individual, conscious thoughts and allowing the spirits of the loas *to enter their bodies.*
Background: A coiled snake, representing the primary Voodoo loas.

VOODOO

Although Voodoo is a separate religion in its own right, incorporating many elements of the prevailing faiths (including Catholicism) of the particular locality in which it is practiced, it has many similarities to the sacred beliefs of West Africa. This is because Voodoo's original practitioners—those who were snatched from Africa and transported across the Atlantic to live in slavery—continued to propagate the sacred beliefs of their African homeland secretly in the New World. While Voodoo is practiced in such African countries as Nigeria and Benin, it centers on Haiti and the Dominican Republic—the slaves' first port of call. It also flourishes in the United States and in Brazil, where the related traditions of Candomblé, Umbanda and Quimbanda are collectively termed Santería, or Macumba.

Reflecting its African roots, followers of Voodoo revere their ancestors, whose spirits are believed to be ever present in this world and who demand respect and homage from their human descendants. Ancestral spirits are just some of those comprising the hundreds of *loas* (deities, whose pantheons are termed *vodu*) that function as the intermediaries between humankind and the remote supreme creator being, named Gran Met. The leading loa is Danbhalah-Wedo, or the "Great Serpent," who is symbolized by a boa constrictor or python, and whose consort is the more delicate, multicolored snake deity Aida-Wedo, called the "Rainbow." Another important loa is Legba, the "Doorkeeper" to the spirit world and, as Maître Carrefour ("Master of the Crossroad"), the loa of sorcery, whose symbol is a cross. Legba is also the sun deity, whose consort is the moon goddess, Maîtresse Erzulie, symbolized by a heart. Furthermore, there are various dangerous deities, collectively termed *guedes,* who are associated with death and sexual excess. One of the most prominent guedes is Baron Samedi, a sinister figure who haunts graveyards and is personified as an undertaker whose face is a skull; phalluses and coffins are his particular symbols. The symbol of each loa may be drawn on the floor of the Voodoo temple (*hounfour*) before a ceremony, inviting the deity's presence at the rite; these ritual drawings are termed *vêves.*

Voodoo rituals are characterized by frenzied drumming, chanting and dancing, intended to drive the participants into a state of ecstasy during which the loas—whose spirits are said to be contained in jars called *govis* which are placed on the *pe* (altar)—will take possession of their human worshippers. Before the rite commences, the master of ceremonies, *la place,* waves his ritual iron sword (*ku-bhu-sah*— "cutting away all that is material") to remove all barriers and allow the loas

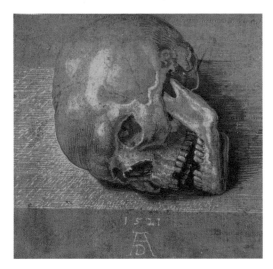

access to their worshippers. To the priests (*houngans*) and priestesses (*mambos*) who preside over the ceremony falls the responsibility of interpreting the loas' wishes as manifested by the behavior of those whom they possess. These officials carry an *asson*: a long-handled rattle fashioned from a calabash, which contains snakes' vertebrae and the eight colored stones that collectively symbolize the ancestral spirits. The rattling sound made when the asson is shaken represents the voice of the loas who have been invoked. During Rada rituals, chickens and goats may be sacrificed to the benevolent loas by their white-clad devotees, in obedience with Danbhalah-Wedo's command to do so, while the violent Petro rites that honor the more sinister loas, or *ge-rouges* ("red eyes"), during which participants are garbed in red, involve the slaughter of pigs.

In common with African cultures, magic and sorcery are important parts of Voodoo. Ailments and misfortune may be attributed to the black magic created by a malevolent sorcerer, or *bokor* ("one who serves the loas with both hands"). The worst fate that can befall the bokor's victim is to be turned into a zombie. This is accomplished when the sorcerer captures the *'ti bon ange* ("little good angel"), the spiritual essence of the person, as opposed to the complementary *gros bon ange*

("great good angel"), which is equated with the life force. After an individual's death, the *'ti bon ange* will linger in the area of the corpse for seven days and may be captured by the bokor while in this state of limbo. If this happens, the corpse will be "resurrected" and forced to slave for the bokor for eternity—a fate clearly dreaded by individuals who were already enslaved in life, and whose only hope for release was death. It is probable that cases of zombiism are the result of victims being drugged into a state of coma resembling death by bokors (who have extensive knowledge of herbalism) and then revived. Voodoo fetishes, or *jujus*—talismans believed to have magical properties or even to be possessed by the loas—both empower and protect the individual against bokors and other evil entities. Another personal charm is the *gris-gris*—a bag filled with magical objects that may be equated to the Native American medicine bundle.

Left: Human skulls and other symbols of death represent the sinister guedes, especially Baron Samedi, who lurks in burial grounds.
Below: Elaborate symbols known as véves are traced on the ground before Voodoo rituals as an invitation to the loas to honor their followers with their presence and participation in the ceremonies.
Background: A coffin, symbolic of the feared Baron Samedi.

Above: *An Australian Aboriginal rock painting depicting a kangaroo. Such indigenous creatures are venerated as totemic ancestors, and tribal members still nurture their strong collective and individual associations with them.*

Background: *A totemic goddess figure carved by fishermen of New Guinea.*

AUSTRALIAN ABORIGINAL SACRED SYMBOLS

According to ancient Australian Aboriginal belief, the world was shaped at the time of the Dreaming, or Dreamtime (altjiranga, in Aranda). Then the first living beings (known as wondjina in the Kimberley region) assumed human, animal, plant, or hybrid form and emerged from the shapeless landmass, or from the primeval waters. They travelled the landscape and, in so doing, created the geographical features of the natural environment—transforming their eyes, for example, into pools of water. The wondjinas did not confine themselves to earthly activities: they also formed the stars and the spirits of the sky and land.

Among the most profound examples of Aboriginal sacred symbolism are the rock, bark and ground paintings that depict these mythical ancestors. Some are convinced that the magical impressions were made by the subjects of the images themselves. Each region has its own specific wondjinas—the rainbow serpents of Arnhem Land, for instance—and local artforms symbolically represent their unique forms. Many Aborigines believe that the wondjinas' supernatural presence is still retained in parts of the landscape, particularly in such sacred places as Ayers Rock (known as Uluru—"great pebble") in the Northern Territory, which is thought to be inhabited by the snake people, hare-wallabies, willy-wagtails and sleepy lizard women who created it.

The Dreaming is a fundamental concept for Australian Aborigines. Its importance stems not only from the fact that it comprises a powerful mythical explanation of the formation of the earth, but also because it continues to inform the sacred ties of kinship, rituals and beliefs of the tribe. For not only did the wondjina shape the landscape, they also laid down every aspect regulating human life, from methods of gathering food, through the correct forms of rites and rituals that ensure the Earth's continuing fertility and bring rain, to social divisions. For example, besides being born into various kinship groups, an individual will belong to one of two tribal groups: either that of the "owner," determined by patrilineal descent; or that of the "manager," or "worker," a status bestowed by virtue of matrilineal descent. Thus the individual's role in tribal rituals will depend on which of the moieties he or she belongs to: "owners," for example, will often direct a ceremony, while "managers" will be responsible for the creation of the ritual art that accompanies it.

Despite their cosmogenic, ordering function, it is usually not these creator beings that hold the positions of immediate importance in Aboriginal sacred belief, but rather the tribal totemic ancestors. Some believe that each person is a reincarnation of his or her totemic ancestor (which may be an animal, plant, or star), and that they thus possess two souls—an individual human soul and a collective totemic soul. The purpose of totemic initiation ceremonies, which are generally performed at puberty, is both to reinforce an individual's personal communion with his or her totemic spirits (and during the ceremony, the initiate will

Left: Aborigines regard Uluru, or Ayers Rock, in Australia's Northern Territory, as a sacred site inhabited by the spirits of participants in the Dreaming, whose enduring presence is symbolized by numerous rock paintings.

Below: Of vital importance to all tribal cultures is the regular performance of ritual ceremonies, each of whose component parts has profound symbolic significance in the context of their sacred beliefs.

receive a totem symbolic of this mystical unity) and to strengthen the sacred bonds that hold the group together. Clearly inherent in the belief in totemic ancestors is the concept that humans are an indivisible part of the collective forces of nature—regardless of its division into species. Therefore, both must be respected and cherished in order to ensure mutual survival. Indeed, once initiated, individuals will be obliged to perform "increase" rituals (fertility rituals associated with their totemic ancestors) for the rest of their lives. Thus, although each person has a direct role to play in totemic rituals, the medicine man holds a special place in the tribe, for he has been specially chosen and empowered by the totemic ancestor (through the insertion of rock crystal into his body) not only to receive visions, but also to heal and, if necessary, punish, by magical means.

Most Australian Aboriginal sacred symbols thus fall into one of two categories: those relating to the Dreaming, such as the representations of the wondjina, and those associated with totemic ancestors. Symbols relating to the latter vary, since they depend on the form that the specific totemic ancestor takes, but they will generally display an unmistakable link: a depiction of a kanga-

roo, for example, will symbolize this particular totemic ancestor. Certain totemic objects also have symbolism sacred to the local community, such as the digging sticks of Central Arnhem Land, with which the totemic ancestors were said to dig water holes, or the tjurnga—a board with shaped ends—of the desert Aborigines, which, when pointed by the medicine man, can cause death. It can also be swung like a bull-roarer—a board whirled at the end of a rope—used in most important ceremonies. This is one of the most powerful Aboriginal symbols, for its sound is believed to be the voice of the totemic ancestor.

Below: Every graceful movement executed by Pacific dancers decked with floral leis helps tell a story with deep significance to the community.
Background: The lizard, a totem animal.

PACIFIC SACRED SYMBOLS

Bull-roarers, along with garamuts (drums) and bamboo flutes, also have an important place in the rituals of Melanesia (which comprises Irian Jaya, Papua New Guinea, the Solomon Islands, Vanuatu and New Caledonia), since all enable the spirits to "speak." Indeed, although Melanesia boasts a variety of sacred traditions, many display similarities to those of Australia's Aborigines. To give an example, many Melanesians believe that the earth was cre-ated and ordered by demas, which can be equated with the Australian Aboriginal wondjina. Again, however, the tribal ancestors (tumbuna), as well as the spirits (masalai) that inhabit animals and such natural features as rivers, have a closer association with the tribe than the demas. Successful intercession of the tumbuna governs both collective and individual mana (material success).

Like Australian Aboriginal totemic ancestors, tumbuna may be symbolized by a specific totemic object drawn from nature, such as a lizard or a shark; in some tribes, as in New Ireland, a specific tumbuna may be represented in the form of a carved wooden figure, or malanggan. Although the tumbuna can appear to a chosen few in dreams and visions, the tribal community also has a vital role to play in their worship. For example, lengthy ceremonial singsings, conducted regularly, invoke the tumbuna by the wearing of sacred masks, dancing, ritual re-enactments and the sacrifice of pigs (which are prized commodities). A central feature of the singsing is the erection of the haus tamburan—a spirit house into which the tumbuna enter and a crucial element in male initiation rites. In all of these rituals, the tumbuna are believed to announce their presence through the sound of bull-roarers, garamuts, flutes and through their manifestation into the sacred masks; all these objects are therefore regarded as possessing unlimited powers and are danger-ous unless ritually controlled. They will often be destroyed after the rite in order to protect the community.

Although they share the concept of mana, Polynesian and Maori sacred beliefs differ substantially from those of Melanesia, most notably in their accounts of how the cosmos came into being. According to Polynesian myth, the creator god Tangoroa caused the heavenly bodies to emerge from primal emptiness

(kore) and darkness (po). Father sky (Rangi or Atea) and mother earth (Papa) gave birth to Tane, god of light and the forests, who separated his parents to bring sunlight to the Earth and created the first human beings. Therefore, Tane is the Polynesians' primary god, and is symbolized both by forests and by birds and insects, which act as his messengers. His powers of fertility are represented by carved male figures (tiki). However, there are many other deities, including Hine, or Hina—the first woman, who is the moon goddess and the patroness of women—or ancestral and local spirits, all of which are collectively termed atua, and which may be represented symbolically by carved stones or totem poles.

The gods are the dispensers of mana to humanity, and the tribal chiefs are blessed with it in a greater degree than their subjects. An elaborate system of tapu (from which the word "taboo" derives), or ritual prohibition, prevails, which must be strictly observed in order to maintain a beneficial level of mana. Reflecting his pre-eminent position, the chief's possessions and person are tapu, as are such sacred sites as shrines (ahus, contained in consecrated walled areas called marae), or infringements of the correct form of any ritual—be it a sacred ceremony of worship, or those prescribed for activities like fishing or canoe-building, whose success depends upon the cooperation of the atua. If an individual violates a tapu, he or she must be purified for their own protection. This ceremony is performed by the tohunga, the tribal "priest," who has been initiated into the sacred knowledge of the atua and who has magical gifts of healing and prophecy. It is he who leads the tribe's sacred rites and rituals, communicating with the atua by means of visions, divinatory practices, or through his carved "god-stick," a symbol of his powers.

Above: Pacific cultures rely upon a plentiful supply of fish for sustenance: thus the activities and equipment of fishermen are subject to specific rituals to avoid the violation of tapu.
Background: The crescent moon, an emblem of fertility.

NATIVE AMERICAN SACRED SYMBOLS

Opposite: A Nootka representation of the sacred thunderbird, whale, wolf and snake; an elaborate ritual headdress from the American Northwest; and a pre-Columbian pipe carving. Right: Intricate representations of tribal spirits carved on a totem pole, usually of sacred cedar wood. Below: Pueblo Kachina dolls like this have an instructive rather than a ritual function. Background: Mythical birds are endemic to Native American belief systems.

Native American traditions have a rich and varied history but, because of the nomadic existence of a number of tribes and also as a result of the incursion of European settlers, the sacred cultures of many Native American peoples experienced substantial changes, in some instances being irrevocably destroyed. However, some of the most powerful beliefs remained unchanged: although their content and symbolism varies from tribe to tribe, certain concepts are regarded as sacred by most Native Americans, such as the existence of a supreme being, and the active mystical interaction of humans with the supernatural world of the spirits, believed to be inherent in the whole of the natural world.

Native American mythical accounts of the creation of the cosmos and humanity are varied. They include the coupling of the earth and sky and the "diving" being who modeled the cosmos from mud taken from the bed of the primeval water, which the culture hero (usually an animal such as a hare or coyote, or a bird such as a raven, but sometimes humanlike, as the Iroquois Ioskeha) then shaped, acting later as a teacher of humankind. Further cosmic myths tell of the creative activities of a pair of hero twins, for example the Algonquian Great Hare and Wolf, who often have conflicting roles; the emergence of humans and animals into this world from other realms, as the Navajo people believe; the ambiguous, and sometimes comic, actions of a trickster figure, which

may again take an animal—coyote, hare, mink—or bird form—raven or blue jay; the emergence of life from the dismembered limbs of a supernatural being; or the spinning of a cosmic web by a spider woman, of which the Pueblo tribes tell. Other Native American peoples, such as the Kwakiutl, believe that they are descended from animals who later became human. All these types of cosmic creators are symbolized in the art and rituals of the tribes that believe they owe both their existence and ways of life to them.

Indigenous animals, birds and plants—not necessarily creator, culture-hero or ancestral figures—often have a special relationship with a particular tribe, and the protective power of these totemic figures is symbolically harnessed in such objects as totem poles, in which carved representations of the spirits important to the tribe are placed in hierarchical order. The mythical, all-powerful thunderbird—the eaglelike generator of thunder, lightning and rain—will often assume a position of supremacy at the top of the totem pole, particularly among Native Americans of the Northwest, and can also be represented by the feathered headdress. Tribal rituals, held at prescribed times, affirm the tribe's collective affinity with these protective spirits and seek to enlist their continuing benevolence.

Certain Native American peoples like the Pueblo tribes have highly developed cyclical rituals, known as calendar rounds, which are performed annually in an attempt to ensure agricultural fertility. Both the creation of the world and progression of the nat-

ural cycle are re-enacted in such rituals as the corn and snake dances, when the assistance of natural spirits like mother corn is invoked. Between the winter solstice and midsummer, the Hopi tribe celebrates the return of its kachina spirits—supernatural ancestral figures having hybrid animal, plant and human form—to the earth. The presence of the kachinas, who intercede between humans and the deities, is symbolized by the wearing of masks that depict the kachinas' various characteristics. The kachinas of the Zuñi are known as koko and can be communicated with by means of prayer sticks topped by fluttering feathers, thought to convey messages to the supernatural realm by means of the wind, or similar rituals. The Navajo invoke their yeis, or "sacred people," through such rituals as Blessingway or Holyway. The purpose of these ceremonies is to restore cosmic harmony, and during the ceremony a chanter will recount the lore of the tribe while supervising the creation of symbolic pictures in the form of sand (or dry) paintings, into which the yeis—who drew the first of the sand paintings in the sky and instructed humans in their creation—enter, thus endowing the painting with their supernatural healing powers. After the ceremony, the painting is ritually destroyed, its purpose having been accomplished.

Right: *Shell and bone ornaments, bead and crested headdresses had ritual significance among the Upper Missouri peoples.* **Below:** *The form of Native American calumets varies among tribes, but these "peace pipes" share the sacred ritual function of communion with the spirits.*

Individuals also have personal guardian spirits that reveal themselves during the course of a vision quest. The vision quest, regarded as an important rite of passage for young men, is preceded by rigorous preparation, including self-mortification. The questor will then withdraw from the rest of the tribe and, if worthy, be rewarded with a vision of his guardian spirit (usually an animal or bird), who will grant the questor limited supernatural powers, along with a unique "spirit song," with which the spirit may be called, as well as a medicine bundle containing such symbolic objects as feathers, tobacco, or herbs, to affirm the newly established totemic relationship. Sometimes the spirits will apprise the young man of his destiny as a medicine man—a tribal healer, visionary and diviner—who will be guided in this role by his guardian spirit. Medicine bundles are also symbols of membership in secret medicine societies or lodges that preserve tribal lore, into which entrants are initiated after their symbolic death and rebirth. One of the most famous such lodges is the Iroquois False Face Society, whose celebrated masks invoke the power of the tribe's totemic spirits.

Once the youth has successfully undergone the vision quest, he is regarded as

Above: *Native American weaving, bead- and basket-work all feature symbolic motifs drawn from sacred traditions, as seen in this detail representing the first man and woman.*

Left: *A Cree moose hunter uses this horn to imitate the call of his prey.*

31

an adult member of the tribe and is entitled to play a full part in its rites. An important symbol of ritual sacred communion with the spirits is the sweat lodge. Its construction takes various forms— from that of a simple tipi to the extremely elaborate Sun Dance lodge—but in most cases it is intended to represent the cosmos, with the axis mundi at its center. The males of the tribe enter the sweat lodge and seat themselves around heated stones over which water is poured to create the steam, or smoke, that connects humans to the spirit realm. The symbolic function of smoke as a form of communion with the spirits is reinforced by the smoking of a calumet, or "peace pipe." The calumet is usually believed to derive from a sacred archetype, such as that given to the Oglala Sioux by the White Buffalo Woman, and is a symbolic microcosm of the cosmos: its clay bowl represents the earth; its wooden stem, plant life; its decorative carving, animals and birds; while the tobacco it holds symbolizes all living things.

Whatever their specific sacred beliefs or the form of their rites, all Native American faiths affirm the holistic nature of the natural world and, therefore, the importance of ritually maintaining the harmonious balance of all its components. Indeed, such is the strength of this fundamental belief that it has survived the disruption and destruction engendered by the European settlement of North America and Canada—often at a terrible price—as well as the later incursions of modern technology and ways of life.

MESOAMERICAN SACRED SYMBOLS

Many Native American beliefs survived despite overwhelming odds. However, those of Mesoamerican religions that had endured since 2300 BC were effectively stamped out by the Spanish conquest. The Aztec civilization that the conquistadors destroyed had absorbed many of the beliefs of the Olmec, classic Mayan and Toltec peoples that preceded it. Of all these religions, the classic Mayan (AD 200–900) was perhaps the most sophisticated. Its main purpose was the enlistment of the support of gods to ensure that the land would remain fertile enough to produce the corn on which the community depended. According to the Mayan view of the cosmos, the heavens were divided into thirteen sections, each ruled over by a specific god such as Ah Kin (the sun); Ix Chel (the moon goddess); Ah Mun (the corn); and the chacs, or rain gods. These deities were presided over by Itzamna, the creator god who first fertilized the universe. His counterpart was Cizin, ruler of the nine gods of the underworld, and it was the balance of conflict between the realms of life and death symbolized by these supreme gods that determined whether there would be drought and famine, or rain and fertility.

Perhaps the most impressive symbols of Mayan worship are the temples constructed on the apex of the huge stepped pyramids that represent the cosmic mountain. Other striking architectural features with profound sacred symbolism are the ball courts, in which participants ritually re-enacted the cosmic struggle between the heavens and the underworld, on whose outcome the fertility of the earth depended. The Mayans also developed a complex written language, the pictographs and ideographs of which symbolized the sacred concepts that dominated everyday life, while their remarkably accurate calendrical system (in which a "month" consisted of twenty days), allocated each day a sacred color, a cardinal direction, a bird and gods of day and night.

Although the Toltecs retained many aspects of Mayan sacred belief, they accorded their war gods pre-eminence over the Mayan fertility deities. The legend of the Toltec priest-king Topiltzin Quetzalcoatl, ruler of the city of Tollan during the Toltec golden age, had an enormous influence on the Aztecs. Topiltzin Quetzalcoatl brought wealth and harmony to his people, but was brought down by the sorcerer Tezcatlipoca, who, with the help of his smoking mirror, caused the king to break his sacred vows. The defeated Topiltzin Quetzalcoatl fled the city and sacrificed himself—either by burning, whereupon he became the morning star, or by sailing away, vowing to return. It was this legend that led some Aztecs to believe that the conquistador Cortés was the "white god" whose return had been promised.

Quetzalcoatl became one of the greatest of the Aztec gods, whose number also included the baleful Tezcatlipoca; Tlaloc, the rain god; Huitzilopochtli, the god of

Opposite top: The symbolic designs that adorn these tipis reflect practical concerns of the Plains tribes and the sanctity ascribed to the natural world.
Opposite below: The webbed dreamcatcher is intended to entrap the positive dreams of such supernatural entities as spider woman, bringing them to bear upon the life of the individual and the tribe. **Below:** *Human sacrifice was a vital part of Mesoamerican sacred ritual, in hope that the gods would receive nourishment from the victim's blood and thus look favorably upon their worshippers. The Aztecs regarded excision of the heart—symbolic of the life force—as efficacious.*
Background: Concentric circles, representing the sun and eternity.

Above: The massive stepped Toltec pyramids at Teotihuacan symbolized the cosmic mountain: at the summits of such pyramids stood temples dedicated to the worship of specific gods.
Background: The powerful and elusive jaguar.

sun and war, who was especially associated with the town of Tenochtitlan, the Aztec capital (today Mexico City); and Ometeotl, the creator god whose dualistic aspect was expressed in the forms of both female and male gods. The carved Calendar Stone (AD 1500) is one of the most comprehensive representations of the complex cosmos of the Aztecs and symbolizes their belief that they lived in the fifth age—that of the sun of movement—which followed the ages of the suns of jaguar, wind, fiery rain and water. The Aztec view of the cosmos placed Tenochtitlan at the center of an Earth surrounded by water. The Earth itself was divided into four quarters, each of which was assigned a symbolic color and influence (like those of the Mayans before them, Aztec cities were constructed in similar quadrants, representing the cosmos in microcosm and thus linking their supernatural and earthly worlds). Each of the thirteen regions of the heavens was accorded a color, as well as a specific bird sacred to its ruling deity.

Representations of their mighty gods dominated Mesoamerican symbolic systems. One of the four children of Ometeotl, Quetzalcoatl was regarded by the Aztecs as the patron of humanity and agriculture. Although, like most divinities, he was sometimes represented in the forms of lesser

gods who symbolized more specific natural powers, he was most often pictured as the "feathered serpent." In this guise, he was frequently depicted in conflict with his brother and sinister opposite, Tezcatlipoca, divine lord of darkness, who was symbolized by his smoking obsidian mirror, which possessed magical properties, and his serpent's foot. The jaguar was sacred to Tezcatlipoca as a symbol of darkness, but because of its associations with cunning and transformation, this creature also symbolized the power of many other gods. Another major divinity was Tlaloc, the rain god, whose powers were often divided among four lesser tlaloques (equated with the Mayan chacs), which ruled over the four cardinal directions. Tlaloc was usually depicted with a face made up of writhing serpents—symbols of lightning and water—and baring his jaguar's teeth. The gift of fertility within his power made him one of the most actively worshipped Mesoamerican gods, but powers of fertility were also embodied in the divine mother of the gods, Tetoinnan, whose various aspects were personified in such goddesses as Xochiquetzal, goddess of love; Tlazolteol, patroness of sexuality; and the terrible mother goddess and hideous devourer, the serpent-skirted Coatlicue.

Although they worshipped many gods whose characteristics were adopted from other Mesoamerican cultures, Huitzilopochtli (who may be identified with Quetzalcoatl), the "hummingbird of the south," was unique to the Aztecs. The perfect warrior, Huitzilopochtli was a divine Aztec culture hero believed to have been born on the site of the cosmic mountain of Coatepec. Later, he led his people to the valley of Mexico where, upon landing in Lake Texcoco, he assumed the form of a golden eagle—a solar symbol. As the god of the midday sun, Huitzilopochtli was symbolized in Aztec art wearing a headdress made either of gold, or of the feathers of hummingbirds (symbols of war). He is sometimes shown carrying the fire serpent Xiuhcoatl, or a shield and arrow. Occasionally, he assumed Tezcatlipoca's smoking mirror and serpent's foot. A great temple (called Templo Mayor by the Spanish, but Coatepec—"snake mountain"—by the Aztecs for their legendary cosmic mountain) was built in his honor in Tenochtitlan. Templo Mayor was a dual shrine, for Tlaloc was also worshipped on this site, thus reconciling a form of sun worship (of Huitzilopochtli) with that of its polar opposite, water. Ritual human sacrifice, usually of prisoners of war, was carried out at Templo Mayor in re-enactment of Huitzilopochtli's slaughter of his 400 siblings (the gods of the south and stellar symbols), as well as his dismemberment of the moon goddess Coyolxauhqui. These rites sought to earn the god's favor and strengthen his power, with which the Aztecs identified themselves. On its dedication in AD 1487, 20,000 prisoners were sacrificed at Templo Mayor, and it is estimated that some 50,000 people were killed there every year.

There were numerous sacrificial methods, but one of the most effective was thought to be the removal of the victim's heart with a flint knife. The victim would be immobilized on a sacrificial stone at the summit of the temple, and, after the heart was removed, the body would be rolled down the steps of the pyramid, symbolizing the descent of the sun. Apart from the significance of human sacrifice as an important aspect of the cult of Huitzilopochtli, it was more generally believed that the blood and hearts of the sacrificial victims nourished all the gods collectively and thus maintained cosmic order. To other gods were dedicated sacrifices appropriate to their characteristics: Tlaloc, for example, would receive young children (symbols of fertility), while the corn goddess would be offered the body of a young girl whose

decapitated head represented the corn cob. Masters of sculpture, the Aztecs decorated their temple complexes with many symbolic images related to sacrifice, including chac-mools—reclining figures representing dead warriors with bowls on their chests to receive the hearts of sacrificial victims.

Despite the powerful beliefs that drove the Aztecs' sacrificial rites, they failed to save their civilization. However, the sacred beliefs of Mesoamerica are immortalized in its richly symbolic artistic legacy.

Below: The supreme Aztec god Huitzilopochtli, pictured with his symbolic attributes of war: the hummingbird headdress, the Xiuhcoatl fire serpent and the feathered shield.

Mediterranean & Northern European Symbols

Like members of tribal cultures, the ancient peoples of Egypt, the Near East, the Mediterranean and northern Europe marveled at, and puzzled over, the natural phenomena that dominated their physical existence. Yet, while the sacred beliefs of tribal cultures remained inseparable from the natural world, the civilizations of northern Africa and Europe went further in developing complex pantheons of gods which not only played a vital role in the regulation of nature, but also were envisaged as leading colorful lives. Indeed, so important were the gods to these civilizations that their sacred symbolism was concerned primarily with the personification of the deities. The advanced civilizations of ancient Egypt, Greece and Rome were founded on sacred principles that controlled every aspect of life; although perhaps less spectacular, the Mesopotamian, West Semitic, Celtic and Norse cultures also revolved around the interrelationship of their gods. The importance of correct ritual behavior in placating these often vengeful deities was paramount, not only to ensure success in this life, but also to win a place in the next. And, as other civilizations were encountered and, in some cases, conquered, elements of the alien religion were adopted and adapted to the conqueror's sacred beliefs, thus resulting in a rich and dynamic syncretic blend.

Opposite: Osiris, lord of the Egyptian underworld, is generally represented as a crowned and mummified figure holding a scepter and flail, the symbols of his authority. Here he is accompanied by the regal Isis, whose thronelike headdress is a hieroglyph of her name, bearing an ankh. Left: The massive scale and detached expression of this classical sculpture resembles Greco-Roman depictions of their aloof Olympian deities, but its symbolic subject is the Nile, which so dominated Egyptian culture, economy and beliefs. Background: The winged sun disk of Egypt.

ANCIENT EGYPTIAN SACRED SYMBOLS

Two natural features dominated the Egyptian's physical world: the scorching sun and the mighty River Nile, whose annual flooding brought fertility to the parched land. Both the sun and the Nile were vital for the preservation of life: should the former fail to shine, or the latter to flood, disaster would strike. Thus although the ancient Egyptians had originally shared the totemic beliefs of their African neighbors, there evolved at Heliopolis a cult of the sun god, Re. This belief system was intended to placate these natural powers and came to dominate the Old Kingdom.

It was believed that Heliopolis marked the spot where the primeval mountain was created from the murky waters of Nun, causing the emergence of the first god, Re (also known as Atum). The sun god then created the male deity Shu (air) and his female counterpart Tefnut (moisture). The pair gave birth to Geb, the earth god, and Nut, the goddess of the sky (whose body was represented as the arch of the heavens), whose children, in turn, were Osiris, Set, Isis and Nephtys. These nine gods comprised the ennead of Heliopolitan belief, in which Re ruled supreme, cross-

ing the sky in his solar boat as a young man in the morning, becoming adult at noon and an older man at night. During the hours of darkness, he traveled through the underworld (often in the form of a ram-headed man), keeping evil at bay before rising to the sky again at dawn.

In symbolic art, Re was sometimes depicted in human form, but his most powerful symbols were aniconic: the stone obelisk, worshipped as a petrified ray of sunshine, which also represented the axis mundi that linked the Earth with the heavens; and the solar disk, often flanked by a pair of falcon's wings, signifying Re's mastery of the heavens. Its numerous rays often culminated in human hands. The solar disk is prominent in Egyptian iconography, frequently appearing as part of the headdress of the gods, or incorporated into amulets associated with creatures regarded as having positive symbolism. Such creatures included: the scarab, or dung beetle, which, because it laid eggs in dung, came to rep-

complex of Karnak. Other royal edifices with profound sacred symbolism were the pyramids, which represented both the primal cosmic mountain and, through their ascending structure and alignment with the stars, a bridge between Earth and the heavens. The combination of the sphinx's leonine body and pharoah's head embodied the union of natural and spiritual power, and this hybrid creature was thus simultaneously a symbol of perfection, protection and the pharoah's might.

The pre-eminence of Re was rivaled by that of another triad, comprising Osiris, Isis and their son Horus. Egyptian mythology tells how the evil Set, jealous of his brother, drowned Osiris in the Nile, then dismembered his body, scattering its parts throughout the world. The inconsolable Isis, Osiris's sister and wife, resolved to recover his body parts, and, with the help of Thoth, the god of wisdom and magic, assumed the form of a bird in order to do so. Having reassembled Osiris's body by magical means, she was able to conceive their son, Horus, the divine infant who, under the fierce protection of his mother, would eventually avenge his father's murder and become pharaoh of Egypt. Thus it was that Osiris, originally worshipped as a god of vegetation because of his mythical role in bringing agriculture

resent regeneration; the scavenging vulture, which symbolized purification; and the cobra, or uraeus, which signified rebirth and protection.

The pharoahs believed that they were the divine sons of Re, linked to him by a lineage traced back through Horus and Osiris to Geb, the first earthly king. When the Theban princes assumed the rulership of Egypt they merged the characteristics of their own patron god of Thebes—Amun—with those of Re, thus creating the god Amun-Re. Amun-Re was regarded as the head of the Theban triad, which also included his wife Mut and their son Khons, who were worshipped at the vast temple

Opposite: Simultaneously an aniconic representation of the sun god, Re, and an axis mundi, the obelisk stood as a petrified ray of sunlight (far left). Re stands in the center of his solar boat (below) with other major deities; his head is that of the scarab beetle which, like the sun, was a symbol of regeneration. The Egyptian sphinx (above), with its lion's body and pharaoh's head, represented protective authority. The hawk-headed Horus (background).
Left and below: *For the ancient Egyptians, the pyramids symbolized not only the cosmic mountain, but also a link between the earthly and heavenly spheres.*
Background: *The vulture.*

Right: Key participants in weighing the hearts of the dead in Osiris's hall of judgement were the jackal-headed Anubis, the scribe deity Thoth, and the monstrous Ammit. *Below:* The reigning pharaoh claimed direct descent from Osiris through Horus: while the pharaoh had temporal authority over his subjects, after death they became subject to Osiris's rule. This representation illustrates their respective roles and relationship, and is freighted with sacred symbols, including the god Thoth (background).

to Egypt, became the lord of the underworld and a symbol of resurrection and immortality. He was depicted as a mummy, symbolizing his death, wearing the white crown of upper Egypt and carrying the scepter (leadership) and flail (judgement).

It was believed that Osiris presided over weighing the hearts of the dead in his hall of judgement to ascertain whether they were pure enough to merit eternal life. During this procedure, Anubis, the jackal-headed god of embalming, who had helped Isis and Nephtys embalm their murdered brother, manipulated the scales, which held the heart in one basket and the white ostrich feather—symbol of Ma'at, the goddess of truth, justice and divine order—in the other. Thoth (represented with either a baboon's or an ibis's head, the curved beak of the latter signifying both the quest

for knowledge and the crescent moon), the inventor of writing, recorded the result, and passed it on to Osiris for his verdict: either eternal life, or a hideous end in the jaws of the terrible Ammit, part crocodile and part hippopotamus.

Other Osirian symbols include the djed pillar, an aniconic depiction of the god's backbone, representing stability, and the tau or "T" cross, a symbol of life. In combination with the oval of Isis, the tau cross became the ankh—a potent symbol that represented such unions of opposites as masculinity and femininity, heaven and earth, air and water; its keylike shape symbolized immortality through its ability to unlock the doors of the underworld.

Although she was Osiris's consort, Isis was a powerful goddess in her own right—a heady synthesis of sorceress and earth

Below: Anubis, the son of Osiris and Isis, helped his mother and aunt embalm the body of his father and was venerated thereafter as the god of embalming and the tomb. He is identifiable by his jackal's head, as the animal was associated with the realm of the dead. **Background:** *The keylike ankh.*

Right: The frog was the attribute of the Egyptian deity Heket, goddess of birth, on account of its many offspring.
Below: Isis depicted in winged form, the guise she assumed to locate the components of Osiris's dismembered body, thus emphasizing both her mastery of the skies and her protective qualities.
Background: The all-seeing Eye of Horus.

mother, whose fascination was such that she was later worshipped by adherents of the Greek and Roman mystery religions. Isis was represented in a number of ways: as a crescent moon, a white sow, or, like Hathor, as a cow—all fertility symbols that signified her position as the supreme mother goddess. She was also depicted as a bird, such as a kite or vulture, representing the form she had assumed to search for Osiris's body parts, or wearing a headdress in the form of a throne—the hieroglyphical spelling of her name. The primary symbol of Horus, the divine child of Osiris and Isis and master of the skies, was the wedjat—the eye of Horus—depicted either as the right eye, representing

the solar power of Re, with which he was associated and whose winged sun disk he shared as a symbol, or the left, signifying lunar power. Like the symbol of the freed human soul, Ba, Horus could also be represented with the head of a falcon—the bird that dominates the skies.

Indeed, the majority of Egyptian deities were personified in hybrid form, the creature with which they were associated symbolizing the primary characteristic of their powers. Thus Heket, the goddess of birth, was associated with the fertile frog; Set, the evil god of darkness, with a voracious black pig; Bastet, the goddess of love and the moon, with an alert cat—its pupils mimicked the waxing and waning of the moon.

MESOPOTAMIAN AND WEST SEMITIC SACRED SYMBOLS

The Near Eastern region of Mesopotamia, the "land between the rivers" (Tigris and Euphrates), was dominated successively by the Sumerians, Babylonians and Assyrians. Although each culture had its own local and national gods, certain strands of belief were common to all, the most important being that humanity's primary function was to serve the gods.

From the time of the Sumerians, the religious life of the city states that comprised Mesopotamian society centered on the temple. In this stepped pyramid or ziggurat—symbolizing the cosmic mountain that emerged from the waters of creation—the city god, represented by a statue, lived with his divine family, nourished by ritual offerings of vegetation and animal sacrifice. Initially, Sumerian sacred belief was disparate, based as it was on the worship of each city's patron deity, but gradually, there evolved a relatively homogeneous belief in a pantheon consisting of seven major gods, each of whom controlled an aspect of nature. These were An, the sky god, and his son Enlil, god of the air and wind (although An and Enlil ruled the gods, Enlil was regarded as pre-eminent, for his storm-bringing powers, which provided both the rain that was vital to human survival in this dry region, and the wind which could devastate the crops); Enki, ruler of the waters; the earth goddess Ninhursag; Utu, the sun god; Nanna, god of the moon; and Inanna, goddess of the morning star—the planet Venus. The lesser gods of the underworld were Nergal (originally a solar god who killed humans with his fiery heat) and the goddess Ereshkigal.

When the Babylonian king Hammurabi assumed the rulership of Sumer, the characteristics of these gods were merged with those of the victorious civilization, An becoming Anu; Enki: Ea, or Oannes, personified in the hybrid form of human and

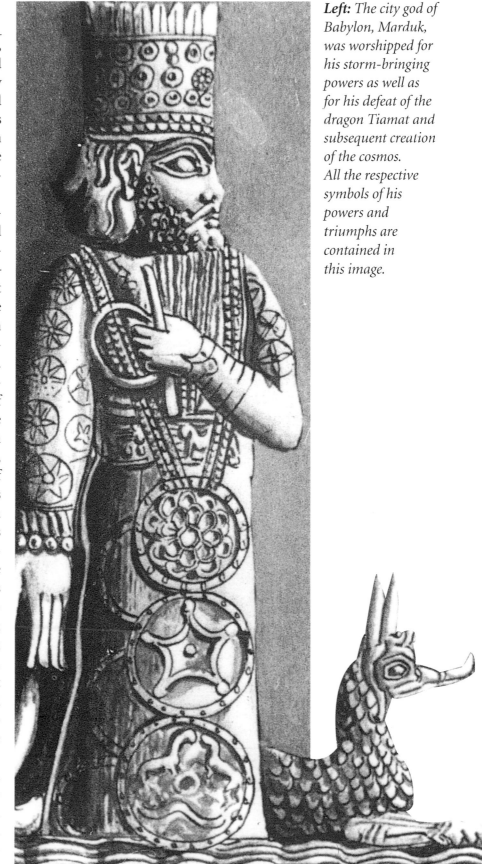

Left: The city god of Babylon, Marduk, was worshipped for his storm-bringing powers as well as for his defeat of the dragon Tiamat and subsequent creation of the cosmos. All the respective symbols of his powers and triumphs are contained in this image.

Right: The eight-pointed star was the primary attribute of Inanna and Ishtar, both of whom were equated with the planet Venus, and of many other Mesopotamian goddesses, including Atargatis and Astarte. Below: The bull was venerated for its strength and virility. Background: The goddess Tiamat, represented as a dragon.

fish; Nanna: Sin; Utu: Shamash; Inanna: Ishtar; and Dumuzi, her lover: Tammuz. The characteristics of Enlil were merged with an important addition to the pantheon, Marduk, the city god of Babylon. The mythological Babylonian creation story, Enuma Elish, relates how he defeated the terrible divine mother and the goddess of salt water, Tiamat (often symbolized by a dragon or serpent), who wrought terrible vengeance on the gods with her demon army after her husband, Apsu—the god of fresh water—was murdered by Ea. Having killed Tiamat, Marduk created the cosmos with her body, and humanity from the blood of her slave, Kingu. The Assyrians, in turn, largely adopted the Sumerian/Babylonian pantheon, but elevated their own national god, Ashur, to a position of supremacy in place of Marduk.

The Mesopotamian gods were often represented in human form, but could also be symbolized aniconically according to their particular overriding characteristics or spheres of influence. Thus the supreme strength of Enlil, the wind god, along with that of Marduk and Ashur, with whom he was identified, could be embodied in the form of a winged bull (an image particularly popular with the Hurrians and Hittites, and one which also symbolized fertility). In recognition of the belief that Marduk had taught the art of agriculture to humans, this god could also be represented by a spade or hoe. Utu/Shamash, the sun god, was symbolized by the solar disk, but because he was the god of justice whose omniscient eye saw all transgressions, the rod of punishment (which also represented rectitude) and a ring, signifying eternity and completion, also became his attributes. Inanna/Ishtar, the Mesopotamian supreme goddess, and the deity of sexual love, fertility and war, was most often symbolized by the eight-pointed star (Venus).

In common with the civilizations of Mesopotamia, agricultural fertility was of crucial importance to the West Semitic peoples, thus explaining the pre-eminence of the wind or storm gods, but also the importance of the earth goddesses. Through trading links, the West Semitic peoples of Syria and Palestine—the Aramaeans, Canaanites and Phoenicians—came to adopt many Mesopotamian gods into their own pantheons. The Aramaeans of Syria, for example, worshipped Shamash, Nergal, Sin and Marduk, but their most powerful indigenous god was the storm god Hadad, whose wife, Atargatis, was equated with the Mesopotamian Inanna/Ishtar, but who also assumed many of the characteristics of the Canaanite goddess of love and war, Anat, as well as of Ashtoreth, or the Phoenician Astarte.

Many individual West Semitic gods became fused into one identity: thus the

Aramaean deity Hadad was paralleled in Canaanite belief by Ba'al (the Philistine Ba'alzebub), son of either the corn god Dagon (who had the form of the fish and became the chief god of the Philistines) or else of the elderly creator deity El—whose strength was symbolized by a bull–and his consort, the mother goddess Asherah. Canaanite myth tells of Ba'al's battles, first with the god of the ocean (Yam) and then with Mot, the deity of death and drought, by whom he was defeated, causing the earth to become dry and infertile. But his warrior sister, Anat (in some versions, his wife Ashtoreth) descended to the underworld and killed Mot, causing both Ba'al and fertility to return to the world. Ba'al's primary symbol was that of the thunderbolt, signifying his power to bring storms, while that of Ashtoreth/Astarte was the cone, signifying the earth.

The West Semitic mother goddess Atargatis, known to the Greeks as "the Syrian goddess," was also an object of wor-ship for some Greco-Roman mystery cults, thus demonstrating the irresistible influence of a particularly powerful deity over cultures that came into contact with the sacred beliefs of alien civilizations. A related cult was that of Mithras—originally an Aryan deity, but one who also had great resonance in Persia—who, in myth, was the divine son/lover of Atargatis. Because the mystery cults were closely ruled by secrecy, many of their beliefs and practices remain unknown, but in the case of the cult of Mithras, which

Above: The barren desert generated many of the sacred symbols of the Mediterranean region.
Below: Although he was a corn god, the Philistines depicted Dagon, their chief deity, with the tail of a fish, perhaps because of piscean associations with fertility.

Right: Pine cones were powerful symbols of fertility in the classical world, and were especially associated with Dionysos, whose thyrsus staff they surmounted, and Attis, whose lover, Cybele, transformed him into a pine tree. **Below, right:** *Crops essential to the survival of the Mesopotamian peoples made grain a major attribute of such mother goddesses as Cybele and Demeter (Ceres), who were believed to control the growth of vegetation.*

Right: A solar-headed female demon, from a Mesopotamian relief.

was especially popular among Roman soldiers, it is believed that he was regarded as a divine solar hero whose slaying and subsequent sacrifice (tauroctony) of the mighty bull was an act of cosmic creation. The Roman cult of Sol Invictus—"the unconquerable Sun," first a Syrian god—shared many aspects of that of Mithras, and in symbolic art the divine duo, both of whom were symbolized by the sun, were sometimes depicted feasting on the conquered bull. Attis, the son and lover of the Phrygian goddess Cybele, also shared the solar symbolism of Mithras and Sol Invictus; like Mithras, he was closely linked with shepherds, stressing his fertility significance, but Attis was frequently associated with Dionysos, too. Cybele—the magna mater—herself became

the focus of a powerful fertility cult, her sexual dominance and elevated status as the mother of the gods prompting the ecstatic orgies that were also a feature of the cult of Dionysos. Like most of the great mothers, her primary symbol was that of the crescent moon, although she was also accorded such attributes of fecundity as corn.

GRECO-ROMAN SACRED SYMBOLS

The adherents of the mystery religions were a minority in ancient Greece and Rome, most of whose citizens worshipped the national pantheon of gods. Through trade and conquest, each of these mighty civilizations was exposed to the gods of other traditions, some of whom were absorbed into their own sacred beliefs—the Romans, for example, adopting the Greek pantheon virtually wholesale, a policy justified by the prevailing belief that the deities of all cultures were inherently the same, although worshipped under different names.

Greek mythology explained how the cosmos came into being through the birth of the gods. Chaos was the original state of affairs, but after the earth goddess Gaia emerged and coupled with her son Ouranos, the god of the sky, the other deities were born. Their Titan son, Kronos, deposed his father and became the supreme god, but was, in turn, usurped by Zeus, his son by Rhea, who, after defeating the Titans, maintained his pre-eminence as head of the Olympian deities. Although the gods were responsible for ensuring that humans followed the moral system of ethike, punishing any transgressions with natural disasters, they generally held themselves aloof from humanity. However, they demanded worship from humans, who erected sanctuaries (temenos) containing statues of their chief gods where they offered placatory sacrifices in homage. Other important forms of worship included festive games, such as the Olympic Games that were sacred to Zeus.

The twelve Olympioi who lived on Mount Olympus were the most important of the Greek gods, and later also became the supreme Roman deities. The Olympian family comprised Zeus (Jupiter), Hera (Juno), Poseidon (Neptune), Demeter (Ceres), Apollon (Apollo), Ares (Mars), Hermes (Mercury), Hephaestos (Vulcan), Athena (Minerva), Aphrodite (Venus), Artemis (Diana) and Dionysos (Bacchus). These gods of the heavens—ouranioi—were supplemented in Greco-Roman belief by deities of the earth—chthonioi—including the lord of the underworld, Hades, and his wife Persephone (Kore), as well as such vicious female demons as the Eumenides (Furies). There were also many other local gods, or lesser gods with specific characteristics, and such supernatural beings as nymphs and muses, plus the semidivine heroes like Herakles (Hercules), Zeus's son by Alcmene, and Asklepios (Aesculapius), Apollon's son and the patron of healing, venerated at special shrines.

Left: Greco-Roman artists depicted their deities in idealized human form and worshipped their images in specially consecrated sanctuaries. This sculpture represents the inscrutable Zeus (Jupiter).

Below: A black-figured amphora ringed by warriors, horses, charioteers and fantastic hybrid creatures.

Background: A hybrid dragon from an ancient papyrus.

Zeus presided over all these divinities. As the ruler of the sky, his primary attribute was the thunderbolt, or staff, with which he manifested his anger; his pre-eminence was also depicted by means of the soaring eagle and the powerful bull; the oak tree, which was thought to attract lightning; and the laurel leaf, the symbol of victory. However, he was also a legendary lover of mortal women, and in this capacity assumed many symbolic forms to seduce the objects of his passion: the white bull that carried off Europa, resulting in the birth of Minos, king of Crete; the shower of gold that impregnated Danae with Perseus; or the white swan to which Leda succumbed, giving birth to Helen as a result. Following Zeus's subjugation of Kronos and the Titans, he retained mastery of the sky, dividing the remainder of the cosmos between his brothers Hades, who received the underworld, and Poseidon, who became master of the sea. Poseidon was symbolized principally by the trident with which he directed the water, but all the sea creatures under his command could also represent him. As Zeus's wife, Hera was the patroness of women, marriage and children, and thus shared many of the attributes of other earth mothers, including Ceres and Artemis. Thus her symbols included those of fecundity, like the multiseeded pomegranate, although the cuckoo (in whose form she was courted by Zeus) and the peacock (which she created from the body of the dead giant Argus,

setting his hundred eyes in its tail) were sacred to her, too. Another sibling of Zeus, Poseidon and Hera was Ceres, mother of the Earth. It was she who held the gift of earthly fertility in her power—a gift which was temporarily withdrawn after her daughter was kidnapped by Hades. Her most important symbol was the ear of corn, but other representations of natural fecundity, such as the pig and the bee, as well as the poppy that represented Persephone's annual return to Hades for half the year, were dedicated to her.

These four gods were the elders of the Olympian pantheon, the other members being second-generation deities. Apollon and Artemis, for example, were the twin children of Zeus by the Titan Leto. Apollon was the god of light and sun, who had received oracular powers from Zeus, and who also presided over the nine muses of the arts. As the sun god, Apollon was symbolized by the solar disk or palm tree, but was also depicted as a charioteer who drove his vehicle across the heavens, or who wielded a bow and arrow as a symbol of his power. As the lord of the arts, he could be represented with a lyre, demonstrating his mastery of music. After killing the python of Delphi, Apollon established his own oracle at the site, transmitting his

prophecies through the Pythoness—the high priestess of the Delphic Oracle—who was widely consulted as she sat on her sacred tripod, itself a symbol of Apollon's wisdom. Further emblems of Apollon include sheep and their shepherds, for Zeus forced his son to work as a herdsman as penance for murdering the Cyclops. Paralleling Apollon's association with the sun, his sister Artemis was identified with the moon, its crescent form being her primary attribute. As the virgin goddess of hunting, she could be symbolized by her weapons—the bow and arrow—and also by animals of the hunt, including the dog,

Opposite: Poseidon (Neptune), above, bearing his three-pronged trident. Artemis (Diana), below, with her bow and arrows (foreground). Background, the laurel wreath, a symbol of victory. **Above:** *The mighty beings of the Greco-Roman pantheon.* **Below:** *Apollon, lord of the nine artistic Muses.* **Background:** *The fruitful pomegranate.*

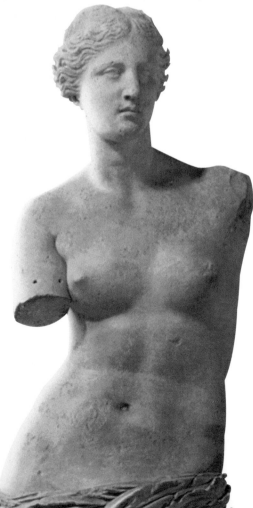

Above: *Botticelli's fifteenth-century masterpiece* The Birth of Venus *illustrates the myth that the goddess was born from the sea and came to shore on a scallop shell, one of her attributes and a symbol of fertility.*
Right: *The immortal Venus de Milo.*

stag and boar, the bear into which she transformed Callisto, or the goat. However, by virtue of her association with the fertility cult of Diana of Ephesus, whose symbol was the bee, this chaste deity could also assume an altogether more earthly nature.

Although not siblings, Ares, the god of war, and Aphrodite, the goddess of love, were linked by their passionate relationship, itself symbolizing the divine reconciliation of opposites. Ares was usually represented bearing his accouterments of war—helmet, breastplate, spear, sword and shield. He was the object of devout worship in the martial Roman Empire, where he was also especially revered as the father of Romulus, the founder of Rome, and Remus. The wolf which suckled the twins, as well as the woodpecker which fed them, both symbolized their father. Ares's lover, the incomparable Aphrodite, was either Zeus's daughter by Dione, or was born from the sea, and, in reflection of the latter myth, one of her

attributes was the scallop shell on which she floated ashore. She was the goddess of sexual love, whose power of attraction was represented by her magical girdle, and she could be represented gazing into a mirror, the symbol of vanity, or surrounded by roses, the flowers of love. She was the mother of Eros (Amor, or Cupid), the mischievous god whose arrows could inflame the heart with love. As Venus, she was the morning star. Symbolized generically by animals, the primary representatives of instinctual behavior, the swallow of spring, the elegant swan, and the cooing dove were sacred to her. Fertility symbols drawn from the natural world, such as the tortoise and the golden apple awarded her by Paris for her sublime beauty, are additional attributes of Aphrodite. As a punishment for refusing Zeus's advances, this promiscuous goddess was married to Hephaestos, the god of fire and metalwork and the lame son of Hera and Zeus. Hephaestos had been instructed in the art of the blacksmith by the Oceanids, and toiled in his fiery volcanic workshops to create artefacts for the

Left and below: Aphrodite (Venus) was the mother of Eros (Cupid, or Amor), portrayed as a cherubic child with a mischievous tendency to fire his arrows of love at the most unlikely targets. Both deities were believed to have power over human passions.
Background: *The apple, sacred to Aphrodite.*

teric wisdom, who assumed particular significance in occult practices. While Hermes embodied the art of cunning, Athena was the goddess of wisdom and war and the patroness of crafts. After her conception by the Titan Metis, her father Zeus, fearing that the unborn child would overthrow him, swallowed Metis and subsequently developed such a terrible headache that he ordered Hephaestos to cleave open his head with an ax, whereupon the fully formed Athena sprang forth. In her martial aspect, she was symbolized by her helmet, spear, and the shield or serpent-fringed cloak known as the aegis, which together represented epheboi, or adulthood. The aegis, fashioned by Hephaestos from the skin of the goat Amalthea, which had nurtured Zeus, was originally an attribute of the supreme god, who produced thunderstorms by shaking it. After Perseus decapitated Medusa with the assistance of Athena's reflective shield, he gave the Gorgon's head to the goddess, who placed it in the center of the aegis. Athena was fre-

Above: Hermes (Mercury), messenger of the Greco-Roman gods, is depicted carrying the infant Dionysos to safety in this third-century mosaic; his winged feet can be seen clearly, but his caduceus has suffered damage.
Right: Athena (Minerva) goddess of wisdom and war, with her attributes: serpent, spear and shield.
Background: The caduceus.

gods, including Zeus's thunderbolts and Apollon's Delphic tripod. His primary symbols were those of fire and the anvil.

The mercurial Hermes was the cunning son of Zeus by Maia, whose ingenuity and mediating skills caused him to become his father's messenger. In artistic representations, Hermes wears a pair of winged sandals, symbolizing his fleet-footedness, and carries the kerykeion ("herald's wand") or caduceus—the snake-entwined, winged staff with the power to convert strife into harmony (in the hands of Aesculapius, it may represent medicine). When amalgamated with the Egyptian god of magic and wisdom, Thoth, Hermes was known as Hermes Tresmegistus, the patron of eso-

the abduction of Persephone by Hades; there members of the cult both mourned her loss and shared her maternal joy upon Persephone's return to Earth. In traditional Greco-Roman belief, Zeus had rescued the unborn Dionysos from the flaming body of his mother, Semele, and subsequently gave birth to the infant from his thigh. Brought up in India in order to protect him from the jealousy of Hera, Dionysos learned the art of wine-making from Silenus and then returned to Greece with the Maenads to introduce his cult at Thebes. He was symbolically represented by both the vine, whose grape causes intoxication, and the phallic-shaped thyrsus—

Left: The owl, with its inscrutable air of wisdom, was a leading attribute of Athena: its nocturnal vision symbolized illumination of the darkness of ignorance by intellectual enlightenment.
***Below:** Caravaggio's seventeenth-century image of the severed head of Medusa, the Gorgon whose terrible stare could literally petrify, and whose crowning glory was a mass of writhing snakes. Athena placed this trophy in the center of the aegis.*

quently depicted in the company of a serpent, the symbol of wisdom, while the owl, whose ability to see in the dark symbolized the penetrative quality of reason, was another of her attributes. Furthermore, it was she who planted the first olive tree (thereby rendering it sacred to her) at the Acropolis in the city of Athens, whose patron goddess she became, and to whom the Parthenon was dedicated.

The twelfth god of the Olympian pantheon, Dionysos, was the focus of a powerful mysteria or mystery cult, one of many such expressions of sacred worship, whose members developed secret systems of ritual and initiation. Although mystery cults were sometimes formed around such "foreign" deities as Mithras, Cybele, Osiris and Isis, certain mysteria were of Greek origin. They included the cult of Demeter at Eleusis, where the goddess was believed to have taken refuge after

Above, left: A Greek vessel depicting the myth of Dionysos's abduction by pirates: the god escaped by transforming his bonds into vines (one of his foremost symbols) and changing his kidnappers into dolphins.

Above, right: The Three Graces, as painted by Peter Paul Rubens.

Right: Numerous lesser spirits were acknowledged in the classical world, including the satyr, whose goatlike physical features symbolized its lecherous nature.

the pine-cone-topped staff entwined with vine and ivy leaves—all symbols of fertility, as were the goats and bulls that were sacrificed to him. The cult of Dionysos emphasized the necessity for attaining the ecstasy that would provide temporary liberation from earthly cares, a state which was achieved through overindulgence in

wine and wild dancing. In addition to being a god of revelry, Dionysos also had a more profound significance—that of resurrection—for not only was he "twice born," but he also traveled to the underworld to rescue his mother.

Although the Olympians were the main focuses of Greco-Roman sacred belief, numerous other deities were also worshipped in both Greece and Rome, including, from the reign of Augustus, the living Roman emperor himself. On the most personal level, the Roman lares, penates, and goddess Vesta—all household deities—were venerated in the fervent belief that the *pax deorum* (the continuing benevolence of the gods) would be maintained as a result.

GERMANO-NORSE AND CELTIC SACRED SYMBOLS

The deities of the pre-Christian Germano-Norse sacred tradition shared many characteristics with those of the Greco-Roman pantheon, as did those of the Celts, albeit to a lesser extent. Thanks to the survival of the Icelandic books of the Edda, Germano-Norse mythology is relatively well documented, while that of the Celts is less well understood—partly because existing documentation is derived from Roman sources, and partly because Celtic sacred beliefs varied from region to region. What is clear, however, is that the outstanding feature of both these northern European belief sytems was the veneration of nature: these deities were worshipped and sacrificed to in sacred groves of trees, as well as at the lakes, streams and hills that they were believed to embody and inhabit. Both cultures also waged warfare, and their ferocious gods were frequently depicted in the midst of battle. Thus both Germano-Norse and Celtic sacred beliefs comprised a potent mixture of mystical communion with nature and martial conflict.

This dual focus is best illustrated in Norse mythology, which featured both a cosmic tree—an evergreen ash called Yggdrasil—and a cosmic battle. Yggdrasil was watered by the eternal spring Urd, which was protected by the three Norns (fates); two other roots led to Niflheim, the realm of the frost giants, and to the land of the giants, guardians of the stream of Mimir, which bestowed wisdom on those who drank from it. As well as supporting the heavens, Yggdrasil contained nine worlds. The most important realm was that of the gods (aesir)—a fortress known as Asgard; humans inhabited Midgard; while the underworld of the dead who did not die in battle was ruled over by a repellent giantess, Hel. A vigilant eagle

lived in an eyrie at the top of Yggdrasil, while a dragon, Nidhogg, lurked at its base. These two wild creatures—one a solar symbol, the other chthonic—exchanged abuse by means of Ratatosk, the mischievous squirrel that scurried between them. The four cosmic stags associated with Yggdrasil represented the winds.

The supreme Norse god was Odin (the Germanic Wotan or Wodan), a deity associated with both military prowess and wisdom. A great fighter, his spear was believed to ensure victory, and this weapon was one of his most important symbols. Others were the eight-legged steed Sleipnir, which carried him into battle; the pair of wolves, Sköll and Hati

Left and below: Living as they did in close harmony with their environment, early northern Europeans believed that the natural features that surrounded them—especially forests—were sacred. Evergreens were particularly venerated, and the Norse cosmic tree Yggdrasil was said to be an ash.

Background: The sky god Thor, whose hammer symbolized his role as the bringer of thunder.

of his children, the most important of whom was Thor (the Germanic Donar)—"the Hurler." A sky god, his primary attribute was his lethal, double-headed hammer, called Mjöllnir, which he hurled in anger and which symbolized the thunderbolt. As well as bringing storms, Thor was the guardian of law and order, and led the *thing*— thc deities' legal assembly. But his primary representation was as a wild, auburn-bearded warrior driving his goat- or ram-drawn chariot across the sky (thus causing thunder). The most popular protective amulets of the Viking age were symbols of Thor: the hammer and the swastika (a solar symbol).

Perhaps the most complex of the Norse gods was Loki, Odin's foster brother. He was a treacherous trickster figure who

Above: Thor as the mighty warrior urging on the goats that pull his chariot across the sky. He brandishes Mjöllnir, source of his thunderbolts.
Right: Freyja, accompanied by fertility symbols and the golden boar.
Background: Leaves and ivy were sacred to the Norse and Celtic peoples.

(representing hatred and repulsion) which accompanied him; and the two information-gathering ravens which sat on his shoulder—Hugin ("thought") and Munin ("memory"). Upon their death in battle, human warriors and kings whose bravery had been outstanding would be conducted by the Valkyries (Odin's female warrior maidens, who were often symbolized by ravens, crows, or swans) to Valhalla, "hall of the slain," where they would be welcomed with a drinking horn brimming with mead. Here the warriors would enjoy a happy afterlife of fighting and feasting, the proceedings presided over by Odin. However, Odin was not only the god of war, but also the god of knowledge, for he had drunk from the stream of Mimir, losing an eye for the privilege; stolen the mead of inspiration from the frost giant Suttung; and acquired the art of writing in runes after hanging in agony from the branches of Yggdrasil.

Frigg (the Germanic Frija) was the goddess of childbirth through her dual role as Odin's wife and mother

fomented conflict between the giants and the gods. It was he who caused the death of the good god Balder (Baldur), the son of Odin and Frigg, by encouraging Balder's blind brother Hother (Hodur) to attack him with a dart of mistletoe—the only plant that had not promised Frigg to protect Balder. Loki was punished for his actions by being immobilized under rocks, paralleling the magical containment of one of his monstrous offspring, the Fenriswolf, or Fenrir. (Loki's other children by a giantess included Hel and the serpent that encircled the world.) According to Norse mythology, the spring thaw was a symbol of nature weeping at Balder's death: thus he was regarded as a fertility god. However, the primary fertility gods were not aesir, but vanir—believed to be supernatural spirits either of the land or of ancestors. The most important were Freyr and his sister Freyja. They were collectively symbolized by golden boars—fecund animals—and by ships. The prolific hare was also a symbol of Freyja, as well as of Holda, the goddess of the moon. The association of these fertility deities with the ship is probably one explanation for the elaborate ship burials discovered at such sites as Sutton Hoo in England, in which the dead, with their worldly possessions, were interred in burial mounds symbolizing their return to the Earth, although a journey to the next world to join their ancestors is also indicated.

Having been created from the body of the giant Ymir, the aesir and humans shared a common origin, and both were constantly threatened by frost giants, symbols of all that was negative in the world. Their dual aim was to steal Thor's hammer and the vanir Freyja in order to gain power over heaven and earth. The final, apocalyptic confrontation came at Ragnorak ("doom of the powers"), when, after a time of bitter cold and chaos, the vengeful Loki led an army of frost giants to attack Asgard.

Accompanying this terrible army were Fenrir and the world serpent. Fenrir devoured Odin, but was then slain by Odin's son, Vidar, while Thor and the serpent, as well as Loki and the aesir Heimdall, fought to the death. The fire giant Surt then ignited the world, which sank into the ocean. Although the gods were dead, Yggdrasil survived to shelter a resurrected world, to which it was believed that Balder would return, and which would be populated by two humans, Lif and Lifthrasir.

The tale of Ragnorak and the subsequent redemption of the world share striking sim-

Below: Celtic crosses are distinguished by the circle that surrounds the arms of the cross. The former is an ancient representation of the dynamic solar wheel: such was its profound and enduring significance in Celtic belief that it was incorporated into the form of Christianity's leading symbol.
Background: *A dragon lived at the foot of the Norse cosmic tree.*

ilarities with the Biblical account of the Apocalypse, illustrating the fusion of pagan beliefs with Christianity. Celtic sacred tradition was similarly influenced, and frequently supplanted, first by the beliefs of the conquering Romans, and then by Christianity. But many Celtic deities, including Brigit (St. Brigid), survived in the form of Christian saints, as did the pagan solar symbol of the wheel, which was retained in the form of the Celtic cross.

Although many Celtic gods displayed similar symbolic characteristics, because they are associated with the local culture heroes of each individual tradition, few can be identified as deities that were worshipped by all Celts. Cernunnos alone is considered an exception to this rule. He was depicted as a cross-legged, antler-horned figure who wore a torc of authority and was surrounded by the animals of

Right: *The Roman goddess Diana was absorbed into Celtic sacred belief and assumed the feminine, lunar attributes of the crescent-shaped sickle and the silver-berried mistletoe.* ***Background:*** *Sea horses, signifying the power of the ocean.*

which he was the master. However, the Dagda, the father of the Irish Tuatha Dé Danaan ("people of the goddess Danu"— an earth goddess) may be equated with the Gaulish god Sucellos (as well as with Thor), for his weapon was a huge club— one end of which could kill and the other revive—which was borne on wheels, thus making it a solar phallic symbol. To him also belonged the cauldron of abundance that nurtured life, and the divine harp which provided music for the gods. Lug, the leader of the Tuatha Dé Danaan, may be associated with Odin, for he shared the Germano-Norse god's attributes of the raven and the victory-bringing spear, as well as his wisdom and mastery of crafts.

The fact that warfare was an inescapable feature of Celtic life is illustrated by the nature of many Celtic gods, and in battle enemies were frequently decapitated and their heads preserved, thus symbolically taking possession of their wisdom and life force. The head cult was a universal Celtic practice, as was the gentler aspect of the sacred inherent in the earth goddess, the counterpart of the horned god. Reflecting the magical and reinforcing power given to the number three, such goddesses as the Irish Danu, Macha and Brigit were often represented in art as groups of three matres or matrones, accompanied by fertility symbols including children, bread and fruit, dogs, birds and trees.

Indeed, the fertile abundance of the natural world inspired most of the Celts' sacred beliefs, rituals and symbols. In Germano-Norse sacred belief, animals like the bull, boar and horse were clearly regarded as having symbolic significance, and this view was shared by the Celts. Thus the Saxon goddess of spring, Eostre (Oestra) was represented by the head of a hare, a fertility symbol; the squirrel was sacred to Mebd; "the Old White One" was Keridwin, the sow goddess; Epona had a horse's head; and the stag was an emblem of warriors and hunter gods. Birds were also attributes and symbols: the raven was sacred to the war goddesses Morrigan and Babd and also personified Bran, whose sister, Branwen, was symbolized by a white crow; swans that wore silver or gold chains were regarded as manifestations of inhabitants of the supernatural Otherworld. Among aquatic creatures, the salmon and trout were particularly sacred, for it was believed that they possessed divine wisdom. The virility of the ram, in conjunction with its spiraling horns, made it a clear solar symbol. When combined with the lunar associations of the serpent, it became a symbol of the horned god Cernunnos, who was depicted as grasping a ram-headed snake in his hand.

Just as the evergreen trees that were ritually burned at the winter solstice (signifying renewal) were symbols of life to the Germanic and Norse peoples, so such trees as the beech, hazel, rowan and yew were sacred to the Celts, for each was believed to possess specific magical properties. The oak tree (which was an attribute of Thor on account of its supposed ability to attract lightning) was especially venerated, and Druids, keepers of the Celtic sacred traditions, swallowed its fruit—the acorn—in the hope that they would absorb its supernatural knowledge. The oak was regarded as male, and the mistletoe which grew on it (said to have been created by a lightning bolt), as female. Its white, translucent berries symbolized the moon. At the winter solstice, mistletoe was cut with a golden sickle (a solar symbol) and caught in a white cloth, thus symbolically freeing the powers of the oak tree.

Despite the fact that many details of Celtic sacred tradition have been lost to us, certain artefacts have survived as enduring testimonies to the beliefs of their creators: for example, menhirs (standing stones), of which the most spectacular grouping is at Stonehenge, in Wiltshire,

England, believed to have been constructed for rituals of solar worship. Menhirs were erected at the site of burial mounds (which, in symbolic terms, can be equated with the cosmic mountain) and may have represented both the tree of life and the markers to the doorways of the Otherworld. And although there is a relative paucity of such man-made symbols, the living symbols of the Celts' most profound sacred beliefs—the various components of the natural world—have continued to flourish over the centuries.

Left: The winter solstice was a high point of the Celtic sacred calendar, when Druids would cut the clinging, "feminine" mistletoe from its host oak tree with a golden sickle and fling it into a white cloth, thus symbolically releasing the oak's masculine strength.

Below: Stonehenge, the ancient stone circle in Wiltshire, England, was constructed as the venue for the performance of sacred rituals so ancient that their exact purpose and content are now unknown.

Background: A Celtic harpist.

The Indian Subcontinent & Asia

Some of the world's most abstract faiths, including Hinduism, Buddhism, Jainism, Sikhism and Taoism, originated in the Indian Subcontinent and Asia, signaling a significant shift of belief from the sanctity inherent in the realm of nature to that of human spirituality. Such religions as these emphasize the importance of the internalization of sacred beliefs—especially of active individual striving for spiritual enlightenment—over the religious traditions in which humans passively accept their peripheral role as lowly subordinates of the omnipotent deities. Buddhism had a particularly strong impact on the civilizations to which it spread, complementing, but not replacing, existing sacred beliefs in, for example, Japan, China and Tibet. However, in countries such as these, many aspects of the old religions survived in peaceful coexistence with the tenets of the new faith, as is illustrated by the transformation of ancient indigenous deities into Buddhist bodhisattvas. Hinduism, however, retained its extensive pantheon of deities relatively unchanged, its similarity to those of many European pagan sacred beliefs testifying to their common Aryan ancestry. Finally, Indian and Asian faiths share many symbols, demonstrating the characteristically pragmatic crossfertilization of sacred concepts in these regions.

HINDU SACRED SYMBOLS

When the conquering Aryans arrived in the Indus Valley, before they reached the Ganges Plain, they found a widespread popular religion that focused on fertility, the objects of worship being the Earth Goddess (Mahadevi) and the components of the natural world. Although elements of this fertility cult were incorporated into the invaders' faith and can be seen to this day in the worship of the goddess (devi), of serpents, or of other spirits of nature, the Aryan religion came to dominate the sacred beliefs of the inhabitants of the Indian Subcontinent, and, indeed, their very way of life.

The thirty-three deities (devas) of the Vedic period, who ruled the earth, atmosphere and sky, are described in the Veda, the three Vedic scriptures. Among the gods of the heavens were the father god, Dyaus; Varuna, the deity of order and the waters, who rode on a makara, a hybrid fish/crocodile; Surya, the sun god; and Vishnu. The chief god Indra, bringer of thunder and lightning, and the wind god Vayu dominated the atmosphere. The earth gods included Agni, the god of fire, messenger of the gods and a bringer of enlightenment, whose vehicle was a ram, a symbol of solar fertility; Yama, the god of the underworld; and Soma, the hallucinogenic-plant deity. From these Aryan gods developed the Hindu deities which still hold sway today.

Opposite: The dome of this Tibetan Buddhist chörten symbolizes the element of fire and is surmounted by a stepped construction, representing the path to spiritual enlightenment. The painted eyes symbolize omniscience and protection, while the fluttering flags are thought to carry believers' prayers to heaven.

Background: A hawk grasping a serpent, representing Vishnu and his mastery of skies and seas.

Left: Hindu representations of goddesses entwined with trees, as illustrated in this bas-relief, derive from the worship of female fertility deities, a feature of the pre-Aryan culture of the Indus Valley.

sacred representations: he has four heads (the fifth was destroyed by Shiva) in order to keep track of his nervously agile consort, Sarasvati, and holds a spoon (signifying sustenance), a necklace and mace (attributes of divine knowledge), a bowl of water (representing fertility), a lotus flower (a cosmic symbol and also one of fertility); and rides a swan or goose, representing wisdom. In terms of the focus of worship, however, Vishnu and Shiva are far more important, and both Vaishnavas and Shaivaites regard the deity they venerate as the sole representative of cosmic power.

Vishnu is the preserver, the benevolent deity who maintains cosmic order, who may be associated with the Vedic Indra. He is usually depicted as having four arms, which hold respectively the conch shell (representing the primal sound, Om); the discus, a solar symbol; the bow and lotus; and the mace, also called dorje or vajra, the symbol of divine knowledge and authority that can be equated with Indra's thunderbolt. His mount is Garuda, an eaglelike bird, which grasps a serpent in its claws to symbolize Vishnu's mastery of both the heavens and of water. Another representational type

Above: The Hindu trinity, or trimurti, comprising Brahma, the creator; Vishnu, the preserver; and Shiva, the destroyer. Prominent Hindu sacred symbols seen here include the conch shell and solar disk of Vishnu (whose attribute the garuda is shown above right), the trident of Shiva, and the white bull, Nandi.
Right: Shiva as Nataraja, the lord of the dance, within a wheel of fire.

According to Hindu belief, the various conflicting elements of cosmic power are reconciled and unified in the trimurti, or trinity—the divine trio of Brahma, Vishnu and Shiva. While Vishnu is the preserver, Shiva represents the destructive power; Brahma's role is that of the harmonizer of the two. However, although he is the creator god, Brahma is not generally worshipped, being regarded as a more abstract divine entity. This view is expressed in the Advaita Vedanta, according to which brahman is the impersonal supreme force in the universe, the ultimate unifying power in which everything is manifested. Nevertheless, Brahma is personified in shows Vishnu sleeping on the coils of the cosmic serpent, Ananta, the symbol of infinity; when he awakes, another universal age is initiated, the new cosmos being symbolized as a lotus that flowers from his navel. Vishnu may also be symbolized in the form of one of his nine avatars, the shapes which he assumed when he descended to earth to save the universe from various evil cosmic threats. Thus he may be depicted as a Matsya (the fish); Kurma the tortoise (or crocodile); Varaha the boar; Narasimba the man-lion; or Vamana the dwarf. His human avatars are Parasurama (Rama with the ax), Rama, Krishna and Buddha. Vishnu as Rama is the hero of the Ramayana, in which he is described as the ideal warrior who, with the help of the monkey god Hanuman, defeated the army of the demon king Ravana, the abductor of his wife Sita; the fall festival of Dasera commemorates Rama's victory. His most popular incarnation, however, is that of Krishna, the god of love, and in this aspect Vishnu is pictured enchanting his paramours, the milkmaids (gopis) of Vrindaban— particularly his great love, Radha—with his flute-playing. A more serious aspect of Vishnu's incarnation as Krishna is his narration of the great moral discourse called the Bhagavad Gita, to the warrior Arjuna. The spring festival of Holi is sacred to Krishna, and is celebrated with the lighting of fires and the throwing of colored water or powder, as is that of Janmashtami, commemorating the deity's summer birthday. Hindus believe that at the end of the present age, known as kali-yuga, Vishnu will be incarnated as the messianic figure of Kalkin, who will ride a white horse.

If Vishnu is clearly a "good god," Shiva's powers are far more ambiguous, comprising elements of the Indus Valley's fertility cult in one of his primary symbols, the phallic lingam, and also the bull-like characteristics of the Vedic god Rudra, with whom he is associated. Although he is known as "the destroyer" and lord of time (mahakala), he

is also the god of creation; indeed, his complex personality is composed of opposing principles, the fact that he can reconcile all these conflicting concepts testifying to his power. Shiva is represented as having a third eye, a dual symbol of enlightenment and destruction, which was created when Pavarti plunged the world into darkness by covering both his other eyes, and as having the matted hair of an ascetic. The goddess Ganga, the divine personification of the river most sacred to Hindus, the Ganges, may be depicted nestling in his hair; the Puranas tells how she fell to earth but was caught in the matted hair of Shiva, whereupon the seven holy rivers were formed. In his hands he may wield the drum that beats the sound of creation, fire, a trident, a bow, and a skull—

*Above: Contemporary dancers enact a scene from the life of Vishnu's avatar as Krishna, the deity of love. Tales of the god's exploits with the milkmaids of Vrindaban, whom he wooed with his skills as a flautist, are much loved, especially those about Radha, who was the reincarnation of his devoted consort Lakshmi. **Background:** The monkey, symbolizing Hanuman.*

Below: *The white bull Nandi (below, right) is venerated in Hinduism not only as the mount of Shiva and the embodiment of masculine potency, but as an emblem of Shiva's evolution from the Vedic fertility god Rudra. Each of the six hands of this goddess figure (below, left) forms a mudra, or symbolic gesture.*

Background: *The boar, one of the avatars of Vishnu.*

symbols of destruction and death—while serpents may entwine his body. His mount is Nandi, the white bull that represents masculine sexual energy and is associated with the crescent moon. As the lord of the dance, Nataraja, Shiva is depicted performing the dance of creation and destruction within a ring of fire, stamping firmly on the body of the dwarf Apasmara (also known as Natesa), who is a symbol of ignorance.

Although Hindu goddesses are generally regarded as inferior to their male consorts, they are the subjects of fervent devotional cults. This is partly a reflection of the worship of the earth mother by the original residents of the Indus Valley, but also because the goddess—collectively and individually—signifies the active cosmic female energy, shakti, the creative counterpart of Shiva's masculine power. While Shiva's sexual power is symbolized aniconically as the phallic lingam, the rounded yoni represents shakti. Shakti is central to Tantric belief, but ordinary Hindus may also worship individual goddesses, particularly Durga, Kali and Pavarti, as the separate manifestations of the various powers of shakti. The ferocious, yet beautiful, Durga is celebrated as the killer of the buffalo demon, and is depicted riding a lion while brandishing such weapons as Shiva's trident. Kali, "the black one," is the terrible goddess of the cremation grounds, whose tongue drips with the blood of her victims, such as the demon Raktavijra, who wears a belt made of severed arms and is draped with a necklace of skulls; in Tantric belief she has ten incarnations. In contrast, Pavarti, the daughter of the mountain god Himalaya, is a benevolent goddess who, after being rejected by Shiva on account

Opposite, top right: A detail from a temple mural dedicated to Sri Maryamman. While the honorific "Sri" is also given to Lakshmi, Maryamman is venerated as a patron of Tamil family life in southeastern India: thus this deity represents the benevolent aspect of the universal Goddess.

Far left: A Nepalese depiction of the elephant-headed Hindu god Ganesha, the patron of prosperity, learning and beginnings, and the remover of obstacles.

Left: The cow is sacred in Hinduism for providing nourishment through its milk: as a symbol of feminine fertility and motherhood, it is equated with the Goddess.

Below: A Hindu temple dedicated to the white elephant, which is venerated by both Hindus and Buddhists, the former for its association with Ganesha, and the latter because Buddha took this form to enter the womb of his mother, Maya. Symbolic lion-dogs protect this sacred site.

of her dark skin, caused her body to glow by means of concentrated asceticism, thus winning the attention of the god. Pavarti is usually depicted in the company of her husband, along with their children Ganesha and Skanda (or Kartikeyya), who battles evil and whose attributes are the spear and the peacock.

Although not as powerful as Shiva's consorts, the lovely, gentle and chaste Lakshmi assumes importance as the loyal consort of Vishnu and as the embodiment of all wifely virtue. Even when Vishnu assumes the different forms of his various avatars, she accompanies him in such incarnations as that of Sita, the wife of Rama.

motherhood—is regarded as sacred in Hinduism, and may not be harmed or its products consumed.

Other important Hindu gods include Ganesha, the son of Shiva and Pavarti. He was given his elephant's head after having been decapitated by Shiva, whereupon his contrite father conferred the leadership of the ganas, Shiva's army of dwarves, upon him. Ganesha's elephantine head symbolizes wisdom, a concept emphasized by his single tusk, for he broke off the other in order to write down the Mahbaharata, the sacred text that contains the Bhagavad Gita. Because he removes obstacles, and because he has a pronounced paunch due to the sweets that he gobbles, Ganesha is regarded as the patron of prosperity (also represented by his consort, Riddhi, or Siddhi) and of beginnings, who is invoked before journeys or business ventures are undertaken. His incongruous mount is the rat (above), whose habit of gnawing underlines Ganesha's ability to solve problems. Hanuman is another hybrid god, having the head of a monkey. He is worshipped in

Above: *Hindu temples are elaborately decorated and incorporate many sacred symbols to invoke protective powers.* ***Right:*** *Hindu ascetics typically devote themselves to Shiva, and emulate him in allowing their hair to grow, daubing their bodies with ashes, and wearing the sign of his third eye on their foreheads.*

Divali, the festival of lights, is sacred to Lakshmi as the goddess of good fortune, and she is welcomed by the lighting of lamps and by the drawing of rangolis— patterns featuring the lotus, which is her favored symbol, for besides representing the cosmos, it also symbolizes fertility and purity. Sarasvati, Brahma's wife and goddess of the arts, is also associated with the lotus, the plant that grew in the river whose form she took. Such is the importance of the collective goddess's powers of fertility that the cow—the milk-giving symbol of recognition of his brave and decisive actions in helping Vishnu's avatar of Rama achieve victory over the demon king.

A central concept in Hinduism, developed in the Upanishads, is that of samsara, in which individuals are eternally reincarnated according to their deeds (karma) unless released by moksha—the unification of the soul (atman) with the absolute (brahman)—which may be achieved by following the correct way of life, known as dharma. The maintenance of dharma includes the devotion to (bhakti), and the ritual worship through offerings (puja) of a dcity, who is not merely personified by a statue or image (murti), but is believed actually to live in it, thus granting the worshipper darshan—the blessing of seeing the god.

Spiritual communion with the deities may also be achieved by meditating on a symbol like the mandala, or on the more abstract yantra, which employs geometric symbols rather than representations of deities. The circular mandala may have Mount Meru, the cosmic mountain, as its central feature, around which the sun, moon and stars revolve. Four continents are depicted on its periphery, along with the protectors of the cardinal directions, the deities Yama, Varuna, Indra and Kubera. (Hindu temples, or murti, may also be constructed according to the cosmic representation of Mount Meru.) Through meditation, the worshipper may penetrate the three levels of such sacred symbols as the mandala to unite ultimately with brahman. Yoga is another important tool in the achievement of enlightenment, of which there are four major forms: karma (ritual), bhakti (devotional), jnana (intellectual), and dhyana (meditational) yoga. In Tantric kundalini yoga, the female energy, shakti, is envisaged as lying in the form of a coiled snake at the base of the spine. Through meditation, the energy can be raised through the seven chakras, symbolized as wheels or lotuses, of the spine until it unites with Shiva, the embodiment of male power, in the head. During meditation specific mantras—words of power—may be chanted. Sound is regarded as having sacred properties, and none more so than that of Om (Aum)—the primal syllable believed to have heralded the manifestation of the cosmos. Its triple vibration symbolizes the states of sleeping, dreaming and awakening, as well as the trimurti.

Above: *Each of the hand gestures, or mudras, of these Balinese dancers conveys a precise message, simultaneously invoking spiritual responses in the observer and telling a story. This symbolic vocabulary comprises hundreds of subtle signs.*
Background: *Yoga practitioners seek unity of body, mind and spirit.*

CHINESE AND JAPANESE SACRED SYMBOLS

China and Japan rejoice in a host of sacred traditions, many of which are interrelated as a result of the sustained historical contact between the two lands, and also because these countries have always been open to the influence of non-indigenous religions, most notably Buddhism. All these belief systems exist in harmony with one another, their respective principles having been pragmatically reconciled.

Foremost among the important Chinese religions are those said to comprise "the three ways" (san-chiao): Confucianism, Taoism ("the way") and Buddhism. Both Confucianism and Taoism place their primary emphasis on the dual nature inherent in all things and the corresponding need to achieve a harmonious balance of the conflicting forces of this duality—yin (the feminine, passive power associated with darkness and water) and yang (yin's masculine, active, solar and atmospheric coun-

terpart). The most powerful symbolic expression of this concept is that of the Taoist t'ai chi, whose circle of unity encloses the equal, sigmoid halves of yin and yang, each of which contains a small circle of the opposite color, representing the fact that each is present in the other and thus demonstrating their independence. The t'ai chi may often be depicted surrounded by the eight pa kua trigrams, whose broken or continuous lines represent yin and yang respectively. The polar forces of yin and yang exist everywhere—within nature, within the human body, and in society—and the purpose of such ancient Chinese systems as feng shui ("wind and water"), a form of geomancy that regulates the form and location of buildings and graves; ch'i, a gentle form of physical exercise; and such oracles as the I Ching ("Book of Changes"), which is based on the sixty-four hexagrams (koua) produced when the eight pa kua trigrams are squared, are all predicated on yin and yang principles.

According to Confucius, human society, too, must maintain a similar balance, and may be guided in this by t'ien, the heavens. Foremost among the vast Chinese pantheon of deities are the chief god, Yu Huang—the Jade Emperor—whose pre-eminence is symbolized by his dragon-embroidered gown and his throne, and Hsi Wang Mu, the "Queen Mother of the West," who rides a white crane and in whose celestial garden grows the peach of immortality. Objects of popular worship are the fu lu shou, the three "star gods": Shou Hsing, the "Old Man of the South Pole" and god of longevity; Fu Hsing, the deity of happiness; and Tsai Shen, god of wealth (or alternatively Lu Shen, the deity of good luck). Lesser gods of special popular importance include Chang Huang, the deity of the cities, and Tsao Chun and his wife, the gods of the stove. Their images are kept in kitchens and are burned—representing Tsao Chun's absence to report on the family's conduct during the year to Yu Huang—and then replaced at Chinese New Year. A leading principle of life which, it is believed, will bring happiness, prosperity and longevity is respect for one's elders, a concept known as filial piety (hsiao), to which the veneration of ancestors (pai tsu) is related. The communication between the living and the dead is symbolized both by the offerings made by descendants and by the ancestral tablets to which prayers are addressed.

Leading Taoist symbols include the image of its founder, Lao Tzu, who is depicted as an elderly wise man, bearing a scroll representing the Tao Te Ching text and riding a water buffalo, the creature that symbolizes both mastery over the animal part of his nature and his legendary journey from his hermitage. Also depicted are the pa hsien, the Taoist Eight Immortals, whose primary collective sign is that of the peach, the symbol of immortality (and thus an attribute of Shou

Left: A Chinese Buddhist mandala of deities. Many indigenous deities were reinterpreted as Buddhist spirits, thus helping to popularize the new faith in China. *Below:* Taoism teaches that the forces of yin and yang are present in nature, so birds and other animals have sacred symbolism. The white crane represents longevity, and is both the special attribute of Hsi Wang Mu and the bird that carries the Immortals to the Western paradise. *Background:* The dragon, signifying good fortune.

Right: The Taoist abbot Lun Yuen. Taoists seek enlightenment and immortality by attempting to harmonize the yin and yang forces within themselves. Below: The peacock may represent the Amitabha and Avalokiteshvara buddhas, as well as the goddesses of mercy Kwan-yin and Kwannon. Background: Tsao Chun, the helpful kitchen god.

Hsing), and also of marriage, of which its Chinese name, t'ao, is a homonym. The Immortals also have individual attributes: the feathered fan of Chung-li Ch'uan; the paper horse of Chang-kuo Lao; the sword of Lu Tung-pin; the writing tablet of Ts'ao Kuo-chiu; the crutch and gourd of Li T'ieh-kuai; the flower basket of Han Hsiang-tzu; the lute of Lan Ts'ai-ho; and the lotus of Ho Hsien-ku.

Reflecting the importance accorded to the natural world, many animals, birds and plants have symbolic significance in Chinese sacred belief. The rabbit (which may also be represented mixing the elixir

of immortality in the moon), deer, crane, mushroom and pine tree, for example, all represent longevity. Jade is associated with immortality, and a significant symbol is that of the pi, a jade disk with a hole bored in the middle which represents heaven. These are all positive (yang) symbols of nature, as are the cock, lion, and tiger, king of the animals. Negative (yin) natural symbols include the five poisonous creatures: the toad, lizard, snake, spider and centipede. In the world of myth, the dragon is a fiercely protective yang being, while both the Chinese unicorn—the ky-lin—and the feng-huang phoenix reconcile yin and yang within their bodies.

Confucianism and Taoism were also integrated into Japan, whose indigenous sacred tradition is that of Shintoism (a word either amalgamated from the Chinese *shen,* "divine entity" and *tao,* "the way," or from the Japanese words *shin,* "belief," and *to,* or "the community"; Shintoism is also called kami no michi ("the way of the kami", which means "sacred being"). The foremost Shinto deity is Amaterasu, the sun goddess and daughter of Izanami and Izanagi, the creator gods of Japan. Amaterasu is represented with a halo of sun rays, holding the necklace presented to her by her father Izanagi when

he made her the ruler of the heavens. Mythology relates that after having banished her brother Tsuki-Yumi, god of the moon, to the night sky, she became irritated by the actions of her other brother Susanowo, deity of storms, and withdrew to a cave, causing darkness to descend upon the world. She was finally enticed from seclusion by the sound of the gods' laughter at the provocative dance of Uzume and the crowing of the rooster, which became sacred to her. Amaterasu is also celebrated as the creator of the rice fields and the patroness of weaving. The Japanese emperor is said to be descended from Amaterasu, and at her royal shrine, Ise-Jingu at Uji-Yamada, are kept the objects collectively known as the go-shin tai. They include the jata-kagami star mirror and the magical sword that Amaterasu is said to have given her great-grandson, the first emperor, Jimmu Tennon.

Deities who enjoy the greatest popular worship include Inari, god or goddess of rice, who may transform him-/herself into an elusive fox, (Inari's primary symbol) and the shichi fukujin ("the seven happiness beings"), who bring good fortune. These are Benten (the eight-armed goddess of the arts and the sea, whose mount is a dragon, and who holds a hoju—magical jewel—sword, key, bow and arrow), Bishamon (the bringer of wealth), Daikoku (the god of wealth who rides a rat, wears a solar disk on his chest and carries a hammer and bags of rice and

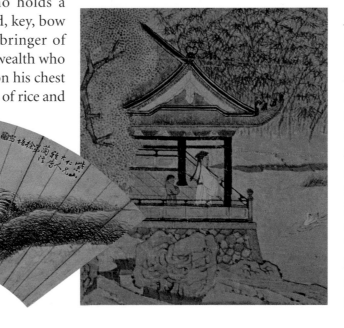

Above: The Japanese Shinto deity Amaterasu is portrayed emanating solar rays, wearing the necklace symbolizing her rulership of the heavens and carrying the imperial sword. **Left:** The faithful enter Shinto shrines through gateways called torii and pray to their deities at haiden, or "worship halls."
Far left: In Japan, fans are regarded as protecting against evil spirits.

jewels), Ebisu (god of work and fishermen, who holds a fish and fishing rod), Fukurokuju, Hotei (god of contentment and the obese bearer of a cloth bag containing riches) and Jurojin (the god who rides a white stag and is accompanied by a crane and tortoise). Images of the shichi fukujin riding in their treasure ship (takara-bune) are often put under children's pillows in the hope that they will have pleasant dreams.

Through his divine descent, the Japanese emperor himself is popularly believed to be a god, but since the Japanese regard themselves as cousins by blood, in venerating their ancestors, they are worshipping

Above: *In ancient Shinto tradition, horses were said to act as messengers between humans and deities. This belief gave rise to the modern custom of offering emas ("horse pictures") to the gods, symbolizing a wish that the gods may grant.*

Right: *The Japanese Cherry-Blossom Dance. The flowering of the sakura tree in early spring heralds the "rebirth" of nature, equating the blossom with prosperity and happiness. Yet because the flower is short-lived, it can also represent a blissful death.*

their divinities. Worship is conducted at shrines, jinja, in which the gods are believed to live, and whose sacred boundary is marked by the torii gateway, traditionally made of three pieces of wood, which symbolizes the right entrance to the sacred way of the gods. The benevolence of the gods may be entreated by means of "horse pictures" (the horse is traditionally believed to be the messenger of the gods) called emas—wooden boards on which a symbol of the blessing required is drawn.

As in China, Shintoism regards the natural world as sacred. Bamboo, plum, cherry, chestnut, pine and willow trees are each believed to be inhabited by deities, as are mountains, whose gods are particularly venerated. Chief among these is Sengen-Sama, the blossom goddess of Mount Fuji (Fujiyama), the sacred center of the Japanese world. Sengen-Sama tends the river of life and may be depicted holding a flower, usually an anemone, camellia, or wisteria (fuji); two other gods are also believed to inhabit Fujiyama: Kuni-Toko-Tachi and O-Ana-Mochi.

Left: *Japanese mythology tells numerous tales of evil demons who prey upon humans, who are helpless without the protection of the gods. The demons' hybrid physical features, as illustrated here, emphasize their ferocity and are in stark contrast to the idealized portraits of the deities.*

Background: *The tortoise, sacred to Shintoism.*

Below: *As the sacred center of the Shinto world, Mount Fuji is one of the most important sites in Japan. It is said to be the source of the water of life, which is guarded by the goddess Sengen-Sama, one of the three deities which inhabit the mountain.*

Below: One of the twelve scenes from the life of Siddhartha Gautama traditionally depicted in Buddhist art is the death of Buddha at the age of eighty, when he was released from the round of existence. Background: The elephant, a sign of Buddha's incarnation.

BUDDHIST SACRED SYMBOLS

Both Chinese and Japanese sacred beliefs were strongly influenced by Buddhism— the religion founded in India by the Buddha, Siddhartha Gautama, between the fifth and sixth centuries BC. The primary symbols of Buddhism are those representing the Buddha himself, as well as the principles he taught to the world.

Legend tells of Siddhartha Gautama's miraculous birth from the side of his mother, Queen Maya: he had been conceived when she dreamed that a white elephant, carrying a lotus, entered her side. Her husband, King Suddhodna of the Shakya dynasty (from whose name is derived Buddha's alternative Mahayanan title, Shakyamuni, "sage of the Shakyas"), cosseted his son, who enjoyed a life of protection and luxury. However, when he was twenty-nine Gautama left the palace, whereupon he had four encounters that would change his life: with a bent old man, with a disease-ravaged man, with a dead body being carried to the cremation grounds, and finally with a saddhu, or ascetic holy man. Profoundly shocked by "the three marks of impermanence" (old age, disease and death) that he had witnessed, Gautama resolved to abandon his life of luxury and follow the life of the saddhu, hoping that he would thus attain enlightenment (nirvana). The harshness of Gautama's new life was in marked contrast to his previously indolent existence, yet after years of fasting to the point of starvation, and traveling through India to sit at the feet of famous teachers, he felt himself no wiser in the quest for spiritual truth. In despair, he finally reached Bodh Gaya, where, sitting under a fig (bodhi) tree, he vowed to stay until he had achieved enlightenment. This he attained after forty-nine days, during which he battled with the evil embodiment of temptation, Mara. Known henceforth as the Buddha ("the enlightened one"), Gautama spent the rest of his life disseminating his spiritual knowledge.

Central to Buddha's teaching of "the middle way" is the importance of following the Buddhist dharma ("the law"), at whose heart lie the "four noble truths": those of suffering (dukkha), the cause of suffering (tanha), the end of suffering (nirvana), and the eightfold path which, if followed, will result in nirvana. In symbolic terms, dharma is represented by the wheel

holding the parasol or canopy of sovereignty over his head). Thus the primary aniconic symbols of Buddhism include footprints (buddhapada), which may be decorated with various representations of the 108 auspicious objects associated with him, such as the lotus (signifying perfect enlightenment, for although it is rooted in mud, it opens into a beautiful flower), whose form may also be equated with the dharma-chakra; Shiva's three-pronged

Left and below: Disciples of the Buddha mourn his death (left), which is followed by his ascension to the Tavatimsa heaven (below). This depiction endows the Buddha with the transcendent serenity that symbolizes his enlightenment.

(chakra) which Buddha is said to have set in motion with his discourse at Sarnath, each of its eight spokes signifying one of the eight "right" (summa) concepts contained in the eightfold path: right understanding and thought, which together result in wisdom; right speech, conduct and livelihood, representing morality; and right endeavor, awareness and meditation, the components of joy.

The dharma-chakra is perhaps the most profound aniconic symbol of Buddhism, but others also represent Buddha himself, as well as aspects of his credo. Many of these were originally Hindu symbols, for just as Hindus recognize Buddha as Vishnu's ninth avatar, Buddha's disciples found little difficulty in reconciling some tenets of Buddhism with those of Hinduism, whose deities were regarded as Buddha's benevolent patrons (illustrated by the fact that Indra is often shown

thirty-two physical attributes (lakshana) which identify "a great man" (mahapurusha) in Buddhist belief, including the monastic robes that represent the ascetic way of life; long, even toes; a halo and bodily aura of spirituality; the urna mark, or tuft of hair in the center of the forehead, signifying a third eye of spiritual vision; elongated earlobes, commemorating the heavy earrings that Gautama wore as a prince; and the ushnisha, a cranial protuberance or topknot symbolizing knowledge. Images of Buddha, which are reverently created according to prescribed methods before being consecrated for worship, generally display all of these lakshana. Another important aspect of the Buddha image is its hand gestures, or mudras. Hinduism recognizes over five hundred mudras, but Buddha is generally depicted as making one of five: both hands joined upward in prayer; making the shape of the dharmachakra; one hand lifted, signifying the dispelling of fear; pointing downward, representing Buddha calling the earth to witness (bhumi sparsha) following his victory over Mara; or with his palms facing upward, symbolizing the bestowing of blessings.

Above: A Buddhist mandala that symbolizes the wheel of life, clutched by Mahakala, the deity of time. At the center are the three creatures that symbolize the cardinal human sins; the central segment is divided into the six realms of existence.
Right: Buddha portrayed in the meditational posture enthroned on the sacred lotus. Background: Ancient emblems of Eastern spirituality: the dharmachakra and swastika.

trident (symbolizing the "three jewels," or ortriratna) of Buddhism; Buddha himself, dharma and the sangha—the enlightened community); the swastika, an Aryan solar good-luck symbol; the royal parasol or flywhisk; and Vishnu's solar disk and conch shell (whose sound represents the voice of Buddha).

Initially, Buddha was symbolized in such aniconic forms, but from the second century AD his physical body began to be depicted, usually engaged in meditation, perhaps seated on a lotus throne in the shade of the bodhi tree ("the tree of enlightenment"), or surrounded by the deer of Sarnath where he preached his first sermon. There are believed to be

The figurative image of Buddha may display these characteristics in sculpture and art, in which scenes from his life may be recreated. Of these, twelve are traditionally significant: Buddha's prehuman existence in the heavenly realm of Tusita; his mother's dream of the white elephant; his birth from Maya's side as she supports herself by means of a tree; his schooling, wedding and other scenes from his royal existence; his rejection of worldly life and his emaciation through fasting; his meditation under the bodhi tree and defeat of Mara; his enlightenment; his sermon at Sarnath; and finally his death (mahaparinirvana), when he is shown reclining on his side. Further sacred images include Buddha seated on the coiled body of the serpent king (nagaraja) Muchalinda, whose seven cobra heads shelter Buddha from the rain, and his incarnation as Maitreya—the future Buddha—a youthful and handsome messianic figure.

Other important Buddhist symbols include stupas: moundlike temples, which in ancient times were the burial sites of royalty, and among eight of which Buddha's remains were said to have been distributed after his death. An architectural representation of the steps of the path leading to nirvana, the stupa is also a cosmic symbol, for it has a square base (representing the earth) and four doors, which signify the cardinal directions. Concentric circles leading to the dome (which symbolizes fire) represent the ascending stages to nirvana, while the spike that surmounts the dome may represent either Buddha himself, nirvana, or the axis mundi/bodhi tree. In Tibet, the stupa takes the form of the chörten, and in Asian countries that of the pagoda. The Buddhist mandala, also a macrocosmic symbol, echoes the form of the stupa. In common with the oral chants of the mantra, the mandala is a meditational tool, which is intended to facilitate the attainment of spiritual enlightenment.

Typical subjects include the forms of Buddha, of which there are many (Gautama is believed to have been the twenty-fourth, while the Buddha Maitreya is yet to come): thus the mandala may contain symbolic images portraying the characteristics of the various Buddhas. It may also represent such Buddhist concepts as the round of existence, which illustrates the six cosmic worlds: those of the gods, dissenting gods, hungry spirits, hell, animals, and humans. At its center are shown the creatures that represent humanity's faults—the snake (hatred), the pig (greed) and the cock (ignorance). Many examples of Buddhist art also include such hybrid animal guardians as fearsome lions, dragons, serpents, or Vishnu's mount, the eaglelike Garuda.

There are a number of Buddhist traditions, but it was Mahayana Buddhism that spread to China and Japan, among

Above and below: Bodhisattvas— compassionate beings who forego nirvana to remain within the round of rebirth in order to help others.

Right: This Theravada Buddhist spirit house—a type of miniature temple—in Thailand has the pagodalike shape that is typical of sacred architecture in much of Southeast Asia.
Background: A Japanese teapot, used in the traditional tea ceremony.
Below: The world's largest, and most spectacular, Buddhist site is that of Borobudur in Java, Indonesia. Built between AD 770 and 850, it combines the symbolic forms of the stupa, the temple mountain and the mandala, representing the Buddhist cosmos.

other countries, following Buddhism's decline in India. One of the most notable ways in which Mahayana Buddhism differs from other schools, such as that of the Theravada Buddhism prevailing in Sri Lanka, Indochina and Thailand, is in its emphasis on the bodhisattvas—"enlightened beings" who have achieved nirvana, but who have chosen to delay their Buddhahood in order to remain with humankind to help end its suffering.

The concept of the celestial bodhisattvas undoubtedly helped Buddhism's assimilation, not only into the sacred traditions of India, but also into those of the Far East, where many indigenous deities became equated with individual bodhisattvas. The characteristics of the benevolent goddesses Kwan-yin and Kwannon of China and Japan, respectively, for example, were merged with the bodhisattva of compassion, Avalokiteshvara (or, more properly, with his female shakti, the white Tara). The Japanese bosatsu Kwannon is represented in one of eight forms, including with the head of a horse (Bato), with eleven human heads (Juichimen), or with a thousand hands (Senju). Jizo, as the patron of children and journeys, is another well-loved Japanese bosatsu, depicted in the garb of a monk, while Vairocana, the Buddha of the sun, may be equated with the Japanese sun goddess, Amaterasu. Further adaptations can be illustrated in China by the transformation of the future Buddha Maitreya into the pot-bellied "laughing Buddha," Mi-Lo Fo, as well as the development of a belief in the eighteen lohans (often confused with Taoism's Eight Immortals), the celestial beings whom Buddha entrusted with the propagation of his teachings after his death, each of whom is depicted as having specific symbolic characteristics. Another aspect of Buddhism's appeal in these countries was related to the impersonal Buddha, Amitabha (the Oriental Amida), whose western paradise, "pure land," or realm of Sukhavati, Chinese and Japanese Buddhists hope to inhabit before achieving nirvana.

Furthermore, Japan evolved its own version of Buddhism, called Zen, from the Chinese school of Ch'an that had been founded by the ascetic teacher Bodhidharma. Both traditions emphasize the spiritual truth contained in the natural world, which may be expressed in the minimalist Zen garden, which unites the power of meditation with that inherent in nature. Further features of Zen, which rejects the worship of an image in favor of spiritual actions and meditation, include calligraphy, which not only records the words of dharma but also unites the calligrapher with Buddha; the tea ceremony, for "Zen and tea are said to have the same taste"; and meditating on the wording of the paradoxical koan riddles.

In Tibet, Buddhism became known as Vajrayana, "the way of the thunderbolt," and this tradition represents a dramatic fusion of Tantric Buddhism with Tibet's indigenous, shamanistic religion, Bon-Po. The primary and eponymous symbol of Vajrayana is the vajra, the staff which represents the thunderbolt that brings enlightenment through skill and compassion, and which was symbolically derived from Vishnu's mace. The vajra has a masculine connotation, particularly when contrasted with the bell, which represents feminine power, wisdom, but also a vacuum; when the two are combined, perfection is attained. The mystical communion attained by chanting mantras (embodied in the sixty-four goddesses of speech) is accorded particular significance in Tibetan Buddhism, whose followers also believe that their supplications are borne to the heavens with the help of the wind. This

belief is manifested either by means of fluttering prayer flags, which are inscribed with invocations, or by prayer wheels—cylindrical drums containing printed mantras—which are spun. There are countless symbolic expressions of Tibetan Buddhist belief, but to Westerners especially, perhaps the most recognizable is embodied in the person of the perpetually reincarnated spiritual leader, the Dalai Lama, who, in his current incarnation in the person of Tenzin Gyatso, has been exiled from Tibet by the Chinese since 1951.

Above: Such elaborate Buddhist images as this bodhisattva surrounded by other celestial beings are intended to draw the observer into the icon, thereby inducing a profound meditational trance in which spiritual truths can be realized.
Background: The staff, or vajra, emblem of Tibetan Buddhism.

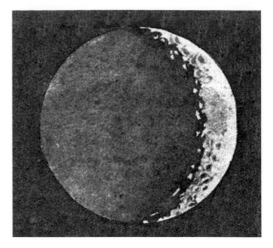

Right and below: Two of the fourteen images that appeared to both of Mahavira's mothers in identical dreams before his birth were the Moon and a vase, each symbolizing an aspect of the future Great Hero's nobility of character. **Background:** *Both concentric circles and the lion (below, right) are symbolic of Jainism.*

JAIN AND SIKH SACRED SYMBOLS

In common with Buddhism, Jainism (or Jaina) and Sikhism are each associated with a historical figure from India: Vardhamana, or Mahavira ("Great Hero"), in the sixth-century BC, and Guru Nanak (AD 1469-1539) respectively. Both sacred traditions arose in reaction to the prevailing beliefs, practices and rituals of Hinduism, especially its sacrificial practices and the caste system that dominated both sacred and mundane life.

Mahavira was a contemporary of Siddhartha Gautama, the Buddha who ultimately rejected the efficacy of ascetic practices in achieving nirvana. Mahavira, by contrast, taught that only by means of the renunciation of worldly life could one attain the enlightenment that would end the eternal round of reincarnation inherent in samsara.

Of the six "great vows," or Mahavratas, that are central to Jainist belief, perhaps the most important is the concept of ahimsa—"not harming." No creature, however humble, may be harmed, for not only can humans be reincarnated into any living form, whether animal, bird, or insect, but violence against one's fellow creatures can result in retributive karma and thus take one further from the merciful release of the soul (jiva), or moksha. For this reason, Jains are vegetarians who may also wear masks to avoid swallowing or inhaling insects and sweep a brush

before them to clear the ground of bugs. Two leading Jainist traditions developed: that of the "sky-clad," (that is, naked, Digambaras, and that of the "white-clad," monastic-robed Shvetambaras.)

Although there are no Jainist gods, there are five levels of "supreme beings" (panca paramesthin): the arhats, "worthy ones," or jinas; siddhas, liberated souls; and, in the human realm, spiritual leaders (acharya); teachers of the Jainist scriptures (upadhyaya); and monks. The five supreme beings may be collectively symbolized in the form of a mandalalike circle, the siddhachakra, in which the central figure of an arhat is surrounded by representations of the other beings. The siddhachakra may be inscribed with the words of the four "jewels" of Jainism: right faith, conduct, austerity and knowledge. The twenty-four jinas ("conquerors"), or tirthankaras ("ford-makers")—of whom Mahavira was the last—are venerated as wise and heroic historical figures whose example leads the way to nirvana, and whose images, if meditated upon, may aid the believer in attaining enlightenment. They are represented in a fashion similar to that of Buddha, and may bear the crosslike srivatsa symbol that represents divinity. According to legend, Mahavira had two mothers: Devananda (who conceived him) and Queen Trishala (his "birth mother"), both of whom, before

Left: *An enormous statue of Lord Bahubali at Shravana Belgola, in India. According to the beliefs of the Digambara sect, he was the first individual to achieve enlightenment and become a siddha. Although he is not a tirthankara, or ford-maker, he is deeply venerated by the "sky-clad."*

Right: The turban is worn by Sikh men as a symbol of devotion to their faith.
Background: The comb, one of the "five Ks," is sacred in Sikhism. Below: The line of the ten Sikh gurus began with Guru Nanak (top left) and ended with Guru Gobind Singh (top right, with family members below). Their collective spiritual leadership endures to this day.

his birth, had fourteen identical, prophetic dreams. These may be symbolized in the form of an elephant, a bull, a lion, the deity Sri, a garland, the moon, the sun, a flag, a vase, a pool of lotuses, a sea of milk, a celestial chariot, a jewel and a smokeless fire. In marked contrast to the asceticism that otherwise prevails in Jainism, the elaborate temples in which such symbolic images may be housed are often highly decorative, representing the beauty that exists in the realm of the enlightened.

Siddhas are symbolized by an empty human silhouette, representing their

achievement of moksha, and the other supreme beings, as monks. Other important Jainist symbols include the round samavasarana, which has a jina at its center from whom concentric circles radiate, signifying the dissemination of the words of the jina's first sermon, and representations of the Jainist cosmos, or loka. Since 1975 the primary symbol of Jainism has been the human hand, represented with its palm facing forward (sometimes with the word "ahimsa" inscribed on it), a sign of peace.

Guru Nanak, the founder of Sikhism, also believed that the path to the Sikh sachkand (release from the cycle of reincarnation) lay in meditation, devotion and service rather than in ritual. He was the first in a line of ten gurus (teachers and those who have communed with Akal Purakh, "the eternal one," or Sat Guru, "true teacher"—God), the last of whom, Guru Gobind Singh, died in 1708. Since then the Sikh community is itself termed a guru (guru panth), as is the Adi Granth (Guru Granth Sahib), the Sikh sacred text. The ten gurus may be depicted in figurative form: Guru Nanak, for example, is often shown holding a meditational mala (rosary) and displaying the solar star on the sole of his foot, representing his elevated status. Scenes from the lives of the gurus may also be recalled through sacred art.

The Sikh community, or khalsa, instituted by Guru Gobind Singh in 1699, established many of the tenets of Sikhism practiced today. Following their initiation (amritsanskar) into the khalsa, a ceremony that includes the sprinkling of holy water (amrit) with a double-edged sword (khanda di pahul), men adopt the last name Singh ("lion") and women that of Kaur ("princess"). From now on, Sikh initiates will follow a strict code of discipline, the Rahit Mayrada. One requirement for men of the Rahit Mayrada is the wearing of the turban, as well as those articles collectively termed the "five Ks" (the initial letter of each of its components). The "five Ks" comprise kes, uncut hair (representing spiritual strength and submission to God); kirpan, a ceremonial sword (with which to fight for truth); kachh, shorts (which symbolize sexual restraint); kangha, a comb worn in the hair (signifying the spiritual discipline suggested by the act of grooming); and kara, an iron bangle (symbolizing union with God) which is worn on the right wrist as a reminder that this hand should be used for good deeds. Although the turban (keski) is not one of the five Ks, it has the dual function of proclaiming adherence to the Sikh faith and symbolizing spirituality and courage.

As well as living according to the principles of their faith, Sikhs worship at the temples (gurdwaras) that house the Guru Granth Sahib. This sacred text is placed on a throne (manji) which is covered with a canopy (both symbols of sovereignty), and while it is being read a sacred chauri, or flywhisk, is flicked over it—another sign of respect for its authority. The most holy of Sikh temples is the Golden Temple (Harimandir—"temple of the Lord") at Amritsar (the site where Guru Nanak was said to have meditated and, since the time

of the fourth Guru, Guru Ram Das, the name of both the city and its sacred "lake of immortality"), which was constructed by the fifth Guru, Guru Arjan.

The Golden Temple is itself one of the most revered symbols of Sikhism, whose foremost aniconic symbol is the khanda, also the word for the double-edged sword that stands at the center of this faith. The sword symbolizes armed protection and belief in God, and its blade is encircled by the chakkar, or steel quoit, which represents variously God, unity and humanity. Two kirpans flank the khanda and chakkar, representing spiritual and temporal power respectively.

Below: A Sikh artistic representation of the Golden Temple of Amritsar, surmounted by the face of its founder, Guru Ram Das. Although the fourth guru excavated the site of the sacred pool Amritsar, the "lake of immortality," the Golden Temple (Harimandir Sahib) itself was finished in 1601 under the direction of his successor, Guru Arjan. Background: The khanda, symbolic of the Sikh warrior-saint.

Religions of the Book

Unlike the wealth of deities and spiritual entities that provide a focus for the sacred beliefs of many other religious traditions, Judaism, Christianity and Islam revere only one supreme being—God (who, although transcending human gender divisions, is generally referred to as "he"). This does not mean that Jews, Christians and Muslims believe that God is the only celestial being—each tradition recognizes that he is assisted by angelic helpers—but, essentially, that there is no other deity to rival or parallel his omnipotence. These three religious faiths may be collectively termed "religions of the book," for each is founded on, and is regulated by, the direct commands from God contained in its sacred texts: the Tanach or Pentateuch (contained in the Torah) of Judaism, the Bible of Christianity, and the Qur'an (or Koran) of Islam. Each religion employs a wide symbolic vocabulary with which not only to represent their God (for most traditions believe that it is blasphemous to attempt to personify him) and to tell the life stories of their prophets, but also to express the concepts contained in their sacred texts. Furthermore, since Jews, Christians and Muslims have all suffered persecution from the dawn of their religions to the present day, their sacred symbols have historically had a dual functions: facilitating the mystical communion with God; and preserving the secrecy of their meanings, thus protecting the symbols and the safety of their followers from the defilement of nonbelievers.

JEWISH SACRED SYMBOLS

The Book of Genesis tells how God created the world in seven days. Initially, God was pleased with his creation, but after the serpent tempted the first woman, Eve, to taste the apple growing on the tree of knowledge in the Garden of Eden, she and Adam were cast out of paradise, thus initiating a chain of increasingly disastrous human actions which would culminate in the wrathful God sending a flood to drown the world. Only Noah and his family were regarded as worthy of surviving this calamity, and the dove that returned to Noah's ark bearing an olive branch and the rainbow that God caused to shine in the sky, are important symbols of both Judaism and Christianity, representing respectively peace and God's covenant with humanity that He would never again destroy the world with such a deluge. Five

Opposite: Surmounting a tombstone, a sculpted angel tenderly clasps a cross, the primary Christian symbol which denotes the eternal life opened to all through Christ's death and resurrection.

Background: The Torah scrolls are sacred as the word of God.

Below: The Creation of the Sun and Moon (1512), a detail from Michelangelo's frescoed ceiling in the Sistine Chapel.

Above: *God's hand animates Adam in Michelangelo's* The Creation of Adam *(1508–12). The pointing index finger is a common motif in Judeo-Christian art and sacred artefacts.*

other individuals received God's covenant on behalf of their people: the patriarch Abraham, the "father of the chosen people"; his son Isaac and grandson Jacob (founder of the twelve tribes of Judaism); Moses, who received the Law from God on Mount Sinai; and David, the first anointed king. The covenants made with these individuals inform the primary symbolism of Judaism.

God's covenant with Abraham, a descendant of Noah, promised Abraham and his heirs the land of Canaan (Israel). As a symbol of this covenant, God commanded that every male be circumcised (as are eight-day-old Jewish baby boys to this day). Yet Abraham and his wife Sarah remained childless until, when Abraham was a hundred years old, the apparently miraculous birth of Isaac was granted them. Among the primary symbolic images associated with Abraham and his son Isaac are Isaac's near-sacrifice by Abraham (known as the *akedah*, or "binding"), and, following his reprieve, that of a ram. The sacrifice of "pure" animals and birds was an important component of ancient Jewish ritual, and, as a test of his unquestioning obedience, God commanded Abraham to sacrifice the much-cherished son of his extreme old age. The sorrowing Abraham was on the verge of complying, when God demonstrated his mercy by sending the archangel Michael to stay his hand. In gratitude, Abraham sacrificed a ram instead. The *akedah* is narrated on the New Year's

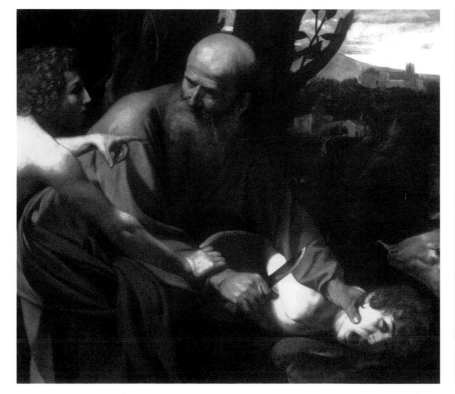

festival of Rosh Hashanah (which commemorates Adam's birthday and may also be equated with an annual—and by extensions, final—day of judgement) as a symbolic reminder of Abraham's demonstration of his devotion to God, and of God's compassion. During this festival, too, the shofar, a hollow ram's horn symbolizing Abraham's sacrifice of the pure ram, is blown to alert transgressors to the need to repent.

Isaac himself became a symbol of martyrdom to those medieval Jews who experienced persecution, while the symbol most often associated with Jacob, who stole his brother Esau's birthright, is the ladder whose rungs angels ascended—a sign from God that Jacob was the heir to God's promise to Abraham. Subsequently, God named him "Israel."

From Moses, whom God commanded to lead his people from slavery in Egypt, derive some of the most significant sacred Jewish symbols, including that which represents God's name. Because it is regarded as too holy to enunciate, (Jewish people speak of it as "the name," hashem), the written name of God, as revealed to Moses, is one of the most profound Jewish symbols, consisting of the Hebrew letters YHWH (in non-Hebrew interpretations, "Yahweh"). The tetragrammaton, as it is known, is often inscribed on amulets or is a central feature

*Right : Moses descending Mount Sinai with the tablets of the Decalogue. His apparent "horns" of light represent his face shining because he had been speaking with the Lord. **Below:** The young David clings to his harp, which is known as his attribute and also symbolizes the Book of Psalms. **Background:** The burning flame reflects God's eternal presence.*

of the *shivviti* plaques that hang on walls in the synagogue and in Jewish homes. It was Moses, too, to whom God gave the Law, the Decalogue (ten commandments) on two stone tablets on Mount Sinai, symbolizing the renewal of his covenant with the Jewish people. On descending the mountain, however, Moses found his people engaged in the idolatrous worship of the golden calf, which caused the text to disappear from the tablets. Moses dropped them in horror, and they smashed. Then he returned to Mount Sinai and engraved two new tablets with the Decalogue himself. It was said that not only could the text be read from both sides, but the letters appeared to hover above the stone. It was these duplicates of the original tablets that were placed in the Ark of the Covenant, along with the fragments of the first set.

The Ark of the Covenant, which housed the tablets of the Decalogue in the sacred area of the tabernacle—and later of the Temple—known as the Holy of Holies, was believed to have miraculous powers. It is recorded as consisting of a gilded wooden box surmounted by a pair of golden cherubim, symbols of God's love, which were said to embrace or to turn away from each other depending on the prevailing level of Israel's devotion to God. After the destruction of the First Temple, the Ark was hidden away, to reveal itself only in the age of the future messiah. Moses is also credited with having created the first menorah, the seven-branched candelabrum that is now a primary symbol of Judaism. Its prototype was said to have been formed miraculously when Moses cast gold into fire; it was fueled by olive oil, and, even if all the other flames were extinguished, one always burned. A symbol of God's wisdom, the menorah's seven branches may represent, among other concepts, the sun, moon and planets, as well as the seven days of creation.

The most prominent symbol of King David is the six-pointed Star of David, or *magen david*, who, it was said, carried a shield in the form of a hexagram against the giant Goliath. Each point of the star may represent a day of the week—or of creation, with the center representing the *Sabbat* (Sabbath). Its interlocking equilateral triangles signify the reconciliation of fire and water, masculinity and femininity, and of the flesh and the soul. It was David's son Solomon who built the First Temple in Jerusalem, David's capital, to house the Ark of the Covenant which David had recovered from the Philistines. During their exile, the Israelites had housed the Ark in the tabernacle, a portable structure; thus its first permanent home was the Temple. The First Temple was destroyed by the Babylonians in 586 BC, and the Second Temple, erected by Herod the Great, shared a similar fate in AD 70 at the hands the Romans, whose savagery initiated the Diaspora, or dispersion of the Jewish people to all parts of the world. The only part of the Second Temple that remains is the western wall, known as the "wailing wall" because it is here that Jewish people still lament their loss. It is believed that the Temple will be rebuilt in the age of the messiah, so the western wall is not only a poignant historical site, but a symbol of the fervent hope for Judaism's future glory.

Although Jewish people honor God in their homes, particularly on the *Sabbat*, communal worship occurs in the synagogue. Here, within the Holy of Holies facing Jerusalem is kept the holy ark (often decorated with depictions of lions, symbolizing the tribe of Judah), a cupboard that contains the sefer torah, or Torah scrolls (two scrolls containing the word of God as set down in the Pentateuch—the first five books of the Old Testament). The sefer torah is hidden behind a curtain (parokhet), symbolizing the division of the sacred from the profane, and is draped with a mantle or enclosed in a wooden case (tik),

as well as being covered with a silver breastplate and topped with two crowns (keter torah, "crown of the Law") surmounted by bells. The text of the sefer torah must be handwritten according to prescribed rules, and may not be touched except with a yad ("hand"), a pointer culminating in a carved hand with a pointing index finger. (The five fingers of the human hand are regarded as protecting against evil, so amulets may also assume this form.) The lamp known as the ner tamid ("eternal lamp") burns constantly above the ark, both as a symbol of God's perpetual presence, and as a reminder of the original menorah, one of whose lights burned always.

Above: *In Titian's* David and Goliath *(1541), the magnitude of David's heroic feat in slaying the giant Philistine is graphically illustrated by the difference in size between the two adversaries. Here David lifts his hands in thanksgiving to God.* ***Background:*** *The menorah, a primary symbol of the Jewish faith and the Israeli state.*

Right: This page from a Kabbalistic manuscript is full of the mystical symbols that are sacred to Judaism, including the menorah, the Star of David, palm trees and human hands.

Below: An eight-branched candelabrum is lit on each successive day during the festival of Chanukkah, to recall the rededication of the Temple by the Maccabees in 165 BC.

Background: The Holy Ark and Torah scrolls represent God's law.

Ritual garments are another important aspect of Jewish worship. Jewish men, for example, wear tefellin ("prayer objects"), or phylacteries—small, black-leather boxes containing four passages of the Law—bound to their left arms and foreheads during the morning shacharit services. These are not only "a sign on your arm" and "frontlet between your eyes," but also serve as reminders of God's extension of his arm over the Jewish people at the time of the Exodus, and of the need to direct all thoughts to God. The four-cornered prayer shawl (tallit, or "cloak"), with tassels (tzitzit) at each corner, symbolizes both obedience to God's commandments and the thread that binds the individual to God, while the wearing of the skull cap (keppel, kipah, or

yarmulke) is both a sign of respect and a reminder of God's presence.

The major Jewish festivals commemorating various aspects of Jewish sacred history are similarly filled with symbolic resonance. Pesach (Passover) celebrates the Exodus from Egypt, during which unleavened bread (matzah)—"the bread of affliction"—is eaten, along with bitter herbs signifying the Israelites' enslavement; a nut, apple, wine and cinnamon mixture in memory of the mortar that they mixed, and salt water symbolizing their tears; green herbs represent spring; while an egg symbolizes sacrifice, as does the roasted bone of a lamb, for the smearing of the blood of the paschal lamb on their doorposts identified the Israelites and saved them during the tenth plague of Egypt. Shavuot ("the festival of weeks") commemorates Moses's receipt of the tablets of the Decalogue, and the blooms that decorate the synagogue recall the flowering of Mount Sinai, while Yom Kippur ("the day of atonement"), which involves the confession of sins and requests for forgiveness, is marked by the wearing of white clothes, symbolizing purity. The erection of tents during Sukkoth ("the feast of tabernacles") recalls the wandering of the Israelites in the wilderness and also features the shaking of a sheaf binding together the arbaah minim ("four species") that represent the four types of Jewish people: the etrog, or citrus fruit; the lulav, or palm; the aravah, or willow; and the hadas, or myrtle. Chanukkah, "the festival of lights," celebrates the victory of the Maccabees over the Selucids and the subsequent rededication of the desecrated Temple in 165 BC, when the menorah burned miraculously for eight days on a single day's supply of oil. A candle is lit each night on an eight-branched candlestick until the eighth evening.

It should also be remembered that by following such commandments as the dietary laws and the keeping of the Sabbat in their everyday life Jewish people are constantly engaged in a living, symbolic affirmation of their covenant with God.

Left: The magen David *("shield of David"), with its many symbolic interpretations, is now one of the leading emblems of Judaism, appearing on the Israeli flag as a symbol of identity.*

Below: A Jewish high priest wearing his ritual regalia, the sacred ephod, *as described in Exodus. The blue gown was fringed with purple, violet and red pomegranates and golden bells, while the breastplate "of judgement" was studded with twelve jewels representing the tribes of Israel, a symbolism repeated in the shoulder rosettes, each of which bore a carnelian engraved with six tribal names.*

Background: The shofar—ram's horn—*symbolizes Abraham's sacrifice of the ram and indicates the need for repentance. The horn is blown on Rosh Hashanah and Yom Kippur.*

Right: Ethiopia, on the Horn of Africa, is the spiritual homeland of the Rastafarian religion. The outlined map of Africa—with the Ethiopian flag colors—itself symbolizes Rastafarianism.

RASTAFARIANISM

Rastafarianism was inspired by black political activist Marcus Garvey's "Back to Africa" campaign, which struck a deep chord with the underprivileged inhabitants of the slum areas of Kingston, Jamaica, during the 1930s. From there it spread to Dominica and other parts of the Caribbean—and later also to Britain—although the wider world became aware of it mainly through the music of Bob Marley and other reggae artists. According to Garvey (1887–1940), the only escape from the grinding poverty and oppression to which people of African origin were being subjected in their Diaspora was by returning to the spiritual homeland of their ancestors, which Rastafarians identify with Ethiopia.

Although Rastafarians do not accept Christianity, their creed is based on the Old Testament and Hebrew scriptures, from which they draw many of their beliefs and their sacred symbols. The cult centers on the charismatic figure of the "Lion of Judah," Prince Ras Tafari (1891 1975)—for whom it was named—who, after becoming the emperor of Ethiopia in 1930, assumed the name Haile Selassie. His coronation was regarded as the fulfillment of an ancient sacred prophecy, and Rastafarians venerate him as their messiah, the incarnation of *Jah* (God) like the Christian Jesus. Those Rastafarians who do not live in the Ethiopian promised land are said to be exiled in Babylon, but, since their messiah has manifested himself in human form, they believe that their redemption is imminent. Thus, Haile Selassie and Ethiopia are the primary symbols of Rastafarianism; other emblems of spiritual unity are drawn from the collective appearance and customs of the faith's adherents.

Rastafarians follow a distinctive lifestyle, which includes the wearing of dreadlocks (in obedience to the Old Testament injunction that hair should not be cut), which are often covered by woolen hats in their traditional colors of red, green and gold. They obey a prohibition against eating pork, salt and shellfish and drinking milk and coffee, in favor of "pure" foods (*I-tal*), and speak a unique dialect to distinguish themselves from nonbelievers. The smoking of *ganja* (marijuana) is extremely important—indeed, a sacrament—for it is said to evoke the mystical feeling of peace that allows the smoker to commune directly with divinity.

Right: Marcus Garvey, originator of the "Back to Africa" campaign on behalf of oppressed blacks descended from slaves brought to the western hemisphere.

CHRISTIAN SACRED SYMBOLS

Christianity shares part of its heritage with Judaism, for both traditions regard the Biblical texts collectively known as the Old Testament as sacred. Yet Judaism and Christianity disagree on a fundamental point: while Jewish people are still awaiting their messiah, Christians believe that he has already manifested himself as Jesus Christ, whose life story and teaching are related in the second part of the Bible, the New Testament. Therefore, the symbolism of Christianity is drawn primarily from the inspirational life of its savior, who led by example and who died to redeem humanity.

The New Testament tells how God chose the Virgin Mary to bear his child by immaculate conception, sending the archangel Gabriel to inform her of her divine mission. In artistic representations of this Annunciation, Mary usually wears a blue cloak, which symbolizes compassion, fidelity and the waters of baptism, as well as a veil symbolizing her modesty. As the white dove that represents the Holy Spirit hovers above, signifying the divine presence, Gabriel holds his messenger's staff, which often takes the form of a lily—a symbol of purity.

Christ's incarnation as a human being is celebrated on Christmas Day, December 25, and his birth in a stable in Bethlehem is commemorated in sacred art as the Nativity. Watched over by his proud mother, the infant Jesus lies in a straw-lined manger, closely regarded by an ox (a creature of service and self-sacrifice which, like the bull, is an ancient symbol of strength), who "knoweth his owner," and who warms the child with his breath, and an ass (which is said to know its master's crib). The three Magi ("wise men," also called "kings"), Caspar, Melchior and Balthazar, who had been alerted to Christ's impending birth by a moving star and traveled from their Eastern lands to worship the new born king, are pictured kneeling in adoration before the child, bearing their costly gifts: gold (representing royalty), frankincense (divinity) and myrrh (suffering and death). Together the Magi may symbolize both the continents of Europe, Africa and Asia and the three ages of humankind: their coming is celebrated at Epiphany, on January 6. The shepherds, too, whom an angel apprised of the divine birth, are present as a reference to Christ's future role as the Good Shepherd who gathers his lost sheep into a single flock.

Many other scenes from Christ's life have been depicted artistically, including his baptism in the River Jordan by John the Baptist, his miraculous feats of healing, his entry into Jerusalem (commemorated with palm leaves on Palm Sunday), or the Last Supper that Christ shared with his disciples.

Left: The resurrected Jesus Christ raises his hand in blessing in this sculpture. Over the centuries, the artistic representation of Christ as a gentle, bearded figure has remained remarkably consistent.

The letters INRI (the Latin abbreviation for "Jesus of Nazareth, king of the Jews") may be inscribed on a scroll above his head. At his feet the three Marys—the Virgin Mary; Mary the mother of James; and Mary Magdalene—may be shown in deep mourning with St. John, called "the beloved disciple." In many Christian traditions, the events of Christ's Passion and death, collectively termed the stations of the cross, are depicted in fourteen pictorial images that hang on church walls.

Although all the instruments associated with Christ's suffering and death, such as the lance with which his side was pierced, the nails that attached his feet and hands to the cross, or the crown of thorns (which, when depicted crowning a skull, signifies eternal damnation) are symbolic of Christ's Passion, it is the cross on which he hung that has become the leading symbol of Christianity. The Latin cross, which can also be equated with the tree of life, may either bear an image of Christ symbolizing his self-sacrifice for humanity, or may be "empty," representing his resurrection. Many other variants of the cross have also evolved, including the shepherd's cross—whose apex takes the form of a shepherd's crook—which symbolizes

Above and right: Both the medieval bas-relief (above) and the paintings at right depict the Annunciation, in which the archangel Gabriel appears to the Virgin Mary to seek her consent to becoming the mother of the son of God. Fra Angelico's angel (detail, near right) bears a lily, symbolizing the Virgin Mary, while the halo—a sign of sanctity— is most prominent in the scene at far right.

Background: The palm stands for the triumphant entry of Jesus into Jerusalem.

However, along with the Nativity, the image of the Crucifixion is paramount both in religious and in symbolic terms. In such images, Christ is depicted in his agony, nailed to the cross, wearing the crown of thorns and bleeding from his five wounds.

Left and below: Scenes drawn from Christ's early life: Botticelli's The Mystic Nativity *(c. 1500), which illustrates the heavenly joy expressed at Christ's birth (far left); the Virgin and Child portrayed in the medium of stained glass (left); and the Christ Child (shown with his symbol, the lamb), Virgin Mary and Joseph (below) in Raphael's* Holy Family *(1505). The depiction of Mary at lower left shows her blue robe of protection, with stars, her attribute.*

Christ as the Good Shepherd (and which has associations with Osiris's scepter) and the cross fitchy, which terminates in a sword, representing willingness to fight for the Christian faith.

The cross was not adopted as an emblem of Christianity until the Council of Constantinople in AD 692: until then, it was considered too graphic to be used as a symbol; additionally, this sign would instantly

Above: John the Baptist by Titian and, above right, by Doré. Christ's baptism with water by John was a symbolic affirmation of His role as savior, and this rite remains the Christian sacrament of initiation.
Right: *Christ carrying the cross to Golgotha. His radiant halo represents divine sanctity.*

identify Christians for persecution by their Roman enemies. Thus the two earliest symbols of Christ and Christianity were the fish, which identified the secret meeting places of Christians in the Roman catacombs, and the labarum. The use of the fish as a Christian symbol has many interpretations: not only did Christ call his disciples "fishers of men," but the Christian fathers termed the faithful *pisculi* ("fish"). Furthermore, besides representing baptism with blessed water, the Greek word for fish, *ichthus,* is an acrostic of the Greek term

"Jesus Christ, Son of God, Savior" (*Iesous Christos, Theou Huios, Soter*). The use of the labarum (also known as the monogram of Christ, the Chrismon, the Christogram, the chi-rho and Constantine's Cross) traditionally dates from AD 312, when, on the eve of the battle of Milvean Bridge, the Roman emperor Constantine saw a vision of a cross in the sky accompanied by the words "*in hoc signo vinces*" ("with this sign comes victory"). Having placed the symbol on his army's shields, Constantine was victorious, whereupon he became a Christian and adopted the chi-rho (so called because the letters from which it is composed, chi (X) and rho (P) are the first letters of the Greek spelling of Jesus Christ) as his emblem.

Other important symbols of Christ include the *agnus dei,* or lamb of god, as St. John the Baptist (whose emblem is also the lamb) called Christ. As well as being a symbol of innocence, the lamb was sacrificed in Jewish rituals as a symbolic wash-

ing-away of sin, and can thus be identified clearly with Christ. The lamb is frequently depicted in association with the banner of the Resurrection, a red cross on a white background. Other creatures with which Christ may be symbolically equated are the pelican, which, it was said, selflessly tore open its breast in order to feed its young, and the dolphin, which was believed to guide the drowning to safety. If Christ is the embodiment of good, evil is personified in the form of the devil (adversary), who tempted Christ three times, and with whom Christ continues to

Above and left: *Although Velázquez's Crucifixion (above) is starker than Raphael's (left), both conform to artistic tradition. Christ bows His thorn-covered head as He gives up His spirit. The mocking sign "INRI" and the wounds of the Passion emphasize His suffering.*
Background: *Christ's emblem, the chi-ro.*

Right and below: Certain animals may represent Christ symbolically, including the sacrificial lamb (below) of the Passover—John the Baptist called Christ the lamb of God (agnus dei)—and the pelican (far right), whose legendary act of self-sacrifice in feeding its young from its breast was compared to Christ's death on the cross to redeem humanity.

Christ is often called the Good Shepherd, who gathers together individual human souls (represented by sheep) and lovingly ministers to His flock, giving it the gift of moral direction and protection. Thus shepherds (near right) symbolize compassionate care for others, as embodied in Christ.

wage war for the salvation of human souls. In this battle, Christ may be represented as the solar eagle, and Satan as the chthonic serpent. Damned souls will be consigned to the fiery realms of hell, where they will endure eternally the torture of the devil's demonic minions, which, like their master, are depicted as hideous hybrid creatures with the goatlike nether regions, including cloven hooves and tails, that symbolize God's enemies.

After his Crucifixion (which is mourned by Christians on Good Friday), Christ rose miraculously from the dead and joined his father in heaven (his Resurrection being celebrated on Easter Sunday). Although God may sometimes be depicted in human form as a wise elder, iconography has traditionally shrunk from attempting to personify the creator. While Christ is depicted in his humanity, and the Holy Spirit as a dove, God the Father is regarded as intangible. Although he may be represented by a ray of light (signifying enlightenment), or as the divine eye which sees all, the most important aniconic symbol of God is that of

the Holy Trinity, which may take the form of an equilateral triangle, three interlocked circles, or the trefoil. Other aspects of God's power may also be represented by angels, spiritual beings who act as intermediaries between heaven and earth. According to Jewish and Christian lore, the triple hierarchy of angels consists of nine orders: seraphim, cherubim, thrones, dominions, virtues, powers, principalities, archangels and angels. Angels, usually depicted in

***Left, opposite and below:** The Holy Trinity of the Father, Son and Holy Spirit is a profound sacred concept in Christianity. Although artists have often been reluctant to portray God figurally, Raphael depicted him as the enthroned Father, enclosed by a mandorla (opposite, below right) who supports his crucified Son. He repeated the motif of heavenly enthronement in a fresco of the Holy Trinity (below). The Holy Spirit is traditionally represented by a dove, which signaled God's forgiveness following the Flood, and, in Matthew's Gospel, took this form when it descended on Christ following His baptism.*

Right: This is an example of one of the many artistic genres in which the Virgin Mary may be represented. Here she gazes down compassionately from heaven, wearing the voluminous blue cloak with which she shelters the faithful, and adorned with a halolike crown of stars. The halo is derived from the solar-rayed coronas of earlier, non-Christian deities, while her stellar attributes were once the emblems of Mesopotamian and West Semitic mother goddesses.

Background: White roses are among the Virgin Mary's attributes, symbolizing love.

Right: The starfish is an attribute of the Virgin Mary as Stella Maris (Star of the Sea), who protects mariners. Its use as a feminine symbol predates Christianity, for in ancient times its starlike shape and aquatic environment associated it with mother goddesses.

beautiful human forms, have wings representing both their spiritual nature and their role as God's messengers. They are often shown making music or singing, representing the divine music that brings harmony. Each of the four archangels who play prominent roles in the Bible has his own symbolic attributes, Michael's sword representing divine judgement; Raphael's pilgrim's staff, divine protection; Uriel's book, divine wisdom; and Gabriel's lily, divine mercy.

Although Mary is not regarded as a goddess, she has a unique status, both because she is the mother of God's son and therefore free of original sin, and as a result of her bod-

ily ascension to heaven (known as the Assumption). She is deeply revered by many Christians, and her symbols include the halo, veil and the blue cloak under which she provides shelter for the faithful (as the Lady of Mercy, Maria Misericord. As the Lady of Sorrows (Maria Dolorosa), her breast is pierced by seven swords. Other potent images of Mary include those known generically as the Virgin and Child, and La Pietà (Lady of Pity), who sorrows over the crucified body of Christ, which lies in her lap.

As Christianity spread throughout the world, the attributes of various pagan goddesses came to be identified with Mary in her status as the primary female figure of Christianity. Thus the crescent moon, the lunar symbol of mother goddesses, and also of chaste goddesses like the Greek Artemis (the Roman Diana), as well as such symbolically associated creatures as the pure-white unicorn and swan, became her attributes. A scallop shell similar to that on which the sea-born Greek goddess Aphrodite (the Roman Venus) floated ashore, which contains the "sacred pearl" (Christ) may also represent Mary. As queen of heaven, she may be crowned with the stars that symbolized the Mesopotamian mother goddess Ishtar and the West Semitic Astarte, an association extended to the starfish (for Mary is also called Stella Maris—"star of the sea"). The thornless white rose, which was a Greco-Roman symbol of love sacred

to Aphrodite and Venus, is another symbol of Mary, who is called "the Mystical Rose of Heaven." One of the leading instruments of devotional meditation—the rosary, or rosarium—is thus a Marian symbol of Christianity (although it is also a feature of many other religions). Traditionally, the rosary consists of fifty or a hundred and fifty small beads strung together into a circle and divided by larger beads into five or fifteen "decades," each of which represents the major events that marked Mary's life. When at prayer, each small bead indicates the recitation of the Ave Maria ("Hail Mary"), and the larger beads, the Gloria and Pater Noster ("Our Father") prayers.

Christ's twelve apostles, the foremost disciples, also have their own symbols. The authors of the Gospels, the Evangelists Matthew, Mark, Luke and John may be represented by (usually winged) tetramorphs ("four signs"), whose images are drawn from descriptions in the Biblical books of Ezekiel and Revelations: Matthew's is a man; Mark's, a lion; Luke's, an ox; and John's, an eagle. Peter is represented by the crossed gold and silver keys to the gates of the kingdom of heaven. Since Peter was the first bishop of Rome, this is also, by extension, the symbol of the papacy. Those who have been canonized as saints by the Roman Catholic Church may be symbolized by those attributes that made them holy: St. Francis, for example, by his stigmata (the bloody marks of Christ's Passion). Martyrs (those who died for their faith) may be represented by the instruments of their death, such as the wheel on

which the body of St. Catherine of Alexandria was broken.

All holy figures, including angels and saints, are depicted in sacred art with halos (aureoles, or nimbi) above their heads. Originally the attributes of pagan solar gods to symbolize sunrays, in the Christian context halos represent sanctity or enlightenment. Although the generic halo is a golden disk or rayed corona, God's halo sometimes has a triangular or diamond shape; Christ's may assume that of the cruciform; and those of living people, such as the pope, may be square (symbolizing the earth). Holiness may also be indicated symbolically by the almond-shaped mandorla (or *vesica pisces*) that surrounds the whole body, representing both the cloud upon which Christ ascended into heaven, and the fish that is his symbol.

Left: Traditional representations of the Virgin and Child, such as this delightful example by Botticelli, depict the Virgin Mary tenderly cradling the Christ Child in her arms. This artistic treatment of mother and divine son can be directly linked to ancient Egyptian images of Isis and Horus, venerating the role of maternal care and nurturing.

Background: The Rosary symbolizes the Virgin Mary.

Left: Each of the four Christian Evangelists is represented by a tetramorphic symbol. The eagle is the attribute of John, as shown in this sculpture by Michelangelo, and lecterns that support the Christian Bible often take the form of an eagle with outstretched wings.

Right and below: In Christian thought, angels are the instruments of God's will and act as links between the heavenly and earthly realms. In artistic depictions they are always represented with wings, and may often be portrayed singing or playing musical instruments, illustrating the belief that the strains of beautiful sound create divine harmony. Musical instruments are signs of worship in Christian art.

The churches (traditionally built in the form of a cross) in which Christians worship are full of sacred imagery. Here, in God's house, the sacraments are celebrated. Protestantism recognizes two sacraments: baptism and the Eucharist (Communion), while the Roman Catholic and Orthodox churches celebrate seven: baptism, confir-mation, the Eucharist (Mass), penance, marriage, the conferral of holy orders and extreme unction (although it is clearly not always practicable to administer the latter in church). The crucifix is usually the focal point of the church, beneath which the altar stands, the three steps that lead up to it symbolizing the Holy Trinity. Because

the altar was used for sacrifice in ancient times, it is a reminder of Christ's self-sacrifice and, because it faces the East, it represents rebirth. The altar is traditionally constructed of wood (symbolizing the cross) and stone (representing the rock of Calvary, where Christ was crucified), while its linen covering recalls Christ's burial shroud. At the center of the altar are kept the holy wine and bread, which together comprise the most important act of Christian worship: the Eucharist, or Thanksgiving. Reception of the Eucharist obeys Christ's injunction to his disciples at the Last Supper to eat the bread that signifies his body and to drink the wine that represents his blood in remembrance of his sacrifice. In obeying this command, communicants actively affirm their covenant with their redeemer.

Left and below: Although Christians may pray to God in any environment, they worship Him collectively in God's House. However elaborate or simple these churches may be, both their structures and their furnishings are replete with Christian symbolism, notably that of the cross.

Background: The ciborium of the Eucharist, a sacrament commemorating Christ's sacrifice, through bread and wine symbolic of His body and blood.

Above: The Hazrat Fatimeh shrine in Iran. Fatima was the daughter of Muhammad and wife of Ali ibn Abi Talib, who became the Shi' as first imam after Muhammad's death.

Right: Despite the fact that Muhammad, like Christ, was a historical figure, he is rarely depicted figurally in Islamic art, which upholds the Judaic proscription of "graven images." In this Western illustration, he is pictured reciting from the Qu'ran and wearing a dagger, which represents his willingness to fight on behalf of Islam.

ISLAMIC SACRED SYMBOLS

Although Islamic tradition accepts such Judeo-Christian prophets such as Moses (Musa) and Jesus Christ ('Isa) as messengers (nabi, or rasul) of God's word, Muslims believe that they were merely the precursors of Muhammad, the only true prophet, for it was he who was the mouthpiece of Allah ("he who is God") in giving humanity the sacred words of the Qur'an, and he who established the Islamic din ("way of life," or "religion").

Muhammad (c.570-c.632) was born in Mecca, Arabia, into the family of Quaraysh, the hereditary guardians of the Ka'ba shrine of Mecca. He was orphaned at the age of six and was subsequently trained as a merchant by his uncle before entering the service of the wealthy widow Khadijah, whom he subsequently married. In a society in which Jewish, Christian and other, polytheistic, religious traditions were practiced, Muhammad felt himself compelled to discover the true nature of Allah, and frequently retired to a cave in Mount Hira (Jabal al-Nur, "the mountain of light") to contemplate this question. Here, in about AD 610, he received his first instructions from Allah—now enshrined in the Qur'an—which the illiterate Muhammad continued to receive until his death, dictating the sacred words via his companions to scribes. Among Allah's instructions were that idols should not be worshipped and that the wealthy should share their riches with their poorer brethren.

Following this, the first revelation, Muhammad spread the word of Allah, but by 622 (by which time Khadijah and his uncle had died) the preaching of the now impecunious Muhammad that there was no god but Allah had become unpopular among the polytheistic Meccans. Thus, he was forced to migrate to Yathrib (later renamed Medina, "the city of the prophet"), whose sympathetic inhabitants (ansar—"the helpers") had invited him to mediate in their feuds. (Muhammad's migration to Yathrib is called the hijra and marks the beginning of the Muslim lunar calendar.) From 623 Muhammad and his followers waged a holy war (jihad) against those hostile to Islam, notably the citizens of Mecca. After six years of warfare, during which Muhammad was himself wounded, he captured in 629, promptly rededicating the Ka'ba to Allah. Having subsequently spread Islam throughout most of Arabia, the prophet made his final pilgrimage to Mecca and Mount Arafat in 632, whereafter he died and was buried at his mosque in Medina.

After Muhammad's death, Islam split into two: the Sunnis chose Muhammad's companion, Abu Bakr, as their spirtual leader, or caliph, and today they follow those of Muhammad's customs (sunna) contained in six texts called the Hadith. The Shi'as (Shi'ites) instead elected Ali, Muhammad's cousin and son-in law, as their imam. A further tradition, known as Sufism, evolved later. Sufism is characterized by the desire for mystical communion with Allah, through such techniques as fasting, or the ecstatic dancing of the "whirling dervishes." One of the most important Sufi symbolic expressions of this desire is that of the simurgh ("thirty birds") to the court of the king of the birds. The lesser birds made an arduous journey to the court on Mount Kaf (the Islamic mythical cosmic mountain). The thirty who were successful in reaching it discovered that they themselves comprised the simurgh, an allegory told in the Persian poem by Farid ad-Din Attar, "The Conference of the Birds."

In obedience to his ban on idolatry, Allah is never represented in any form in Islamic art. Muhammad is not now depicted in figurative art, but because he was a historical personage, his human form was once shown in manuscripts only, with his face hidden behind a veil. The scenes of

Muhammad's life that were illustrated in this way include the descent of the archangel Gabriel (Jibr'il) to the cave in Mount Hira and his exhortation to Muhammad to "recite (iqra) in the name of Allah." Islam shares the Jewish and Christian hierarchies of angels (including the fallen angel Lucifer, or Memnoch, whom Christians call Satan and Muslims Iblis, or Shaytan), and these are also represented with haloes and wings. Muhammad is generally depicted wearing a green mantle and encompassed by a fiery halo in artistic representations of such momentous events as his night journey, when he traveled on his mythical, human-headed horse, al-buraq ("lightning") from Mecca to

Above: *Islamic art is exquiste in its attention to detail, and particularly in its use of geometric and vegetal designs. Until around the fifteenth century, artists adhered strictly to the prohibition against portraying living creatures, but powerful rulers often commissioned representational illustrated manuscripts to enjoy in private.*

Background: *Birds are symbolic of Sufism.*

105

Temple Mount (Haram) in Jerusalem, from which he ascended through the seven heavens into the presence of Allah. Thus the Dome of the Rock that was erected later on Temple Mount is one of the most sacred sites of Islam, and the rock is said to bear the imprint of Muhammad's footstep. Nearby is the Masjid al-Aqsa mosque, where it is believed that humans will be judged on the day of judgement.

As the final resting place of Muhammad's mortal remains at the Mosque of the Prophet, and the site of the Mosque of the Two Qiblas (where Muhammad first

Below: The Hegira, Muhammad's epic spiritual journey, is central to Islamic belief.

turned to Mecca to pray), Medina is also a significant holy place in Islam. But the most sacred city is Mecca, where the cube-shaped Ka'ba, toward which Muslims must turn when praying, stands within the Masjid al-Haram mosque. Muslims believe that Allah instructed Abraham and his son Ishmael to erect the Ka'ba over the site of Adam's legendary sacred sanctuary, and the area known as the Maqam Ibrahim, between the Ka'ba and the Gate of Peace, is believed to mark the place where Abraham stood to supervise its construction. Within the southeastern corner of the Ka'ba, he set the black stone (possibly a meteorite) which Gabriel first gave to Adam (originally white, its present color is said to reflect the transgressions of humanity). Next to the Ka'ba is the Hijr, the spot identified as the burial place of Ishmael and his mother Hagar. The shrine was subsequently desecrated by the Meccans, who worshipped hundreds of deities, and it was Muhammad who restored it to Allah, making it a symbol of his commitment to Allah and reaffirming his status as the final prophet.

On entering the Masjid al-Haram mosque through the Gate of Peace, pilgrims (who must wear a white cloth, the ihram, indicating their purity) enter the sacred area around the Ka'ba, the Mataf. There they perform the tawaf, circling the Ka'ba and the Multazam—the wall adjoining it—seven times (the number of perfection) in an anticlockwise direction. Leaving by the Gate of al-Safa, they run back and forth between the hillocks of al-Safa and al-Marwa (Mounts Cana and Marnia), seven times recalling Hagar's quest for water. On the eighth day of their pilgrimage, they must travel to the Mount of Mercy (Arafat) to present themselves before Allah. Making a pilgrimage—Hajj—to Mecca during Dhu al-Hijja, the twelfth month of the Islamic calendar, at least once during one's lifetime is the fifth of the Five Pillars of Islam that regulate Muslim life. The first pillar is the affirmation of faith contained in the text of the Shahada: "There is no god but Allah and Muhammad is his messenger" (the words embroidered on the kiswa, the cloth that covers the Ka'ba, which also introduce the daily call to prayer, the adhan). The second is Salat—the five daily prayers (at dawn, midday, afternoon, sunset and evening). Fasting during the month of Ramadan—Sawm—is the third pillar, and a reminder of those who live in poverty, while giving alms to the poor forms the fourth pillar, Zakat. The Five Pillars may be symbolized in the form of a human hand, known as the Hand of Fatima (Muhammad's daughter by Khadijah), which may also represent the hand of Allah—itself a Shi'ite symbol.

Ideally, Muslims should perform their five daily prayers at the mosque (masjid, "place of prostration"), to which they are called from the minaret, the tower that flanks it, by the muezzin. Before entering, worshippers must purify themselves by

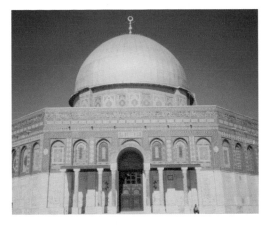

washing in a fountain within the courtyard that encloses the mosque. The architecture of the mosque reflects a symbolic cosmic pattern: its square base represents the Earth, its dome (if built in domical form) the celestial realm, and its minaret (which may be regarded as an axis mundi) and internal columns (if it is a hypostyle mosque), the soaring desire for unity with Allah. After cleansing themselves, Muslims enter the mosque to perform their prayers. They must face Mecca as they worship Allah, and the direction (qibla) is indicated by the mihrab (the empty

Left: The Dome of the Rock in Jerusalem is said to mark the site from which Muhammad ascended to heaven. The spherical dome symbolizes the heavenly realm and is a feature of many mosques.

Below: Sufi whirling dervishes dance ecstatically in order to commune mystically with Allah.

Right: *The Indian-Islamic architectural style of Hunuman's mausoleum in Delhi combines the structural simplicity of the Islamic mosque with the more decorative approach of Mughal art. The building's dome represents the heavenly sphere, while the square form of its foundations symbolizes the Earth.*

Right: *The many calligraphic traditions in Islam include the* naskhi *and* rukah *styles; reproduced here is an example of Kufic script, which is characterized by both its elaborate decorative beauty and its formal composition. Through such exquisite calligraphy, the writer is praising and amplifying the beauty of Allah's message to Muslims.*

niche that focuses the mind on Allah, which may also symbolize the cave at Mount Hira). The mihrab, the minbar (the pulpit from which the preacher, the khatib, delivers his sermon on Friday, the day of assembly) and the kursi, the stand on which the Qur'an is placed, usually comprise the mosque's only furnishings. Worshippers prostrate themselves on the carpeted floor, or on the individual prayer mats (sajjada) that symbolize a clean space, which may be decorated with vegetative or geometric designs in a style similar to that of the walls.

In accordance with the proscription on representing human figures (thus competing with Allah as creator), the usual forms of sacred decorative art include the beautiful, flowing Arabic calligraphy (of which there are many styles) that spells out the sacred texts from the Qur'an. Indeed, the text of the Qur'an (whose name means "recitation" in recollection of Gabriel's command to Muhammad to recite) is among the primary symbols of Islam (its verses are called ayat, "signs"). Abstract geometric patterns and floral and vegetal arabesques may also decorate the fretwork, tiles, mosaics and textiles of the mosque, symbolizing the sacred laws of nature and the garden of paradise respectively.

Although not directly associated with Muhammad, the symbol most closely associated with Islam today is the hilal, or star and crescent, which represents sovereignty and divinity, as well as concentration, openness and victory. The adoption of this symbol is traditionally believed to derive from the waxing moon whose brilliant light saved Byzantium from the attack of Philip of Macedon in 339 BC. Thereupon, the grateful citizens of Constantinople (Istanbul) adopted the crescent moon of Diana as their civic symbol (when the city became Christian in 30BC, the symbol became associated with the Virgin Mary). Sultan Osman had a vision of a crescent moon before his conquest of the lands now known as Turkey in 1299, and it became the emblem of his Ottoman dynasty, to whose scion, Mehmed II, Constantinople fell in 1453. The star was added to the crescent moon in 1793 by Sultan Selim III (possibly because the Ka'ba is said to lie directly beneath the Pole Star), its points being set at five in 1844. From its origins as a dual symbol of the city of Constantinople and of the Ottoman sultans—the secular leaders of the Islamic world who made it their capital—the hilal evolved into a universal symbol of Islam.

Above: *The complex use of geometric patterns that is such an important characteristic of Islamic art celebrates the natural laws created by Allah that regulate the universe.*

Left: *The* hilal, *or star and crescent, is today the universal symbol of the Islamic religious community.*

INDEX

Page numbers in **boldface** refer to illustrations.

BIBLIOGRAPHY AND SOURCES

Norman Bancroft Hunt, *Native Americans: The Life and Culture of the North American Indian*, Chartwell Books, Edison, N.J., 1996.

Anne Baring and Jules Cashford, *The Myth of the Goddess: Evolution of an Image*, Penguin Arkana Ltd., Harmondsworth, 1993.

Udo Becker (ed.), *The Element Encyclopedia of Symbols*, Element Books Ltd., Shaftesbury, 1994.

Robert E. Bell, *Women of Classical Mythology: A Biographical Dictionary*, Oxford University Press, Oxford, 1991.

John Bowker, *World Religions: The Great Faiths Explored and Explained*, Dorling Kindersley, London, 1997.

Cottie Burland, *North American Indian Mythology*, Chancellor Press, London, 1996.

Joseph Campbell, *The Mythic Image*, Princeton Univesity Press, Princeton, N.J., 1974.

Wally Caruana, *Aboriginal Art*, Thames & Hudson Ltd., London, 1993.

Richard Cavendish (ed.), Mythology: An Illustrated Encyclopedia, Macdonald & Co. (Publishers) Ltd., London, 1991.

Jean Chevalier and Alain Gheerbrant, *The Penguin Dictionary of Symbols*, Penguin Books Ltd., Harmondsworth, 1996.

J. E. Cirlot, *A Dictionary of Symbols* (rev. ed.), Routledge, London, 1995.

Roger Cook, *The Tree of Life: Image for the Cosmos*,

Thames & Hudson Ltd., London, 1974.

J. C. Cooper, *An Illustrated Encyclopaedia of Traditional Symbols*, Thames & Hudson Ltd., London, 1978.

———(ed.), *Brewer's Book of Myth and Legend*, Helicon Publishing Ltd., Oxford, 1995.

G. Duchet-Suchaux and M. Pastoureau, *The Bible and the Saints*, Flammarion, Paris, 1994.

David Fontana, *The Secret Language of Symbols: A Visual Key to Symbols and Their Meanings*, Pavilion Books Ltd., London, 1993.

Sir James Frazer, *The Golden Bough*, Wordsworth Editions Ltd., London, 1993.

Clare Gibson, *Signs and Symbols*, Saraband Inc., Rowayton, Conn., 1996.

Marija Gimbutas, *The Language of the Goddess*, Thames & Hudson Ltd., London, 1992.

Rosemary Goring (ed.), *The Wordsworth Dictionary of Beliefs and Religions*, Wordsworth Editions Ltd., Ware, 1995.

Miranda J. Green, *Dictionary of Celtic Myth and Legend*, Thames & Hudson Ltd., London, 1992.

Rosemary Ellen Guiley, *Encyclopedia of Mystical and Paranormal Experience*, HarperCollins Publishers, New York, 1991.

James Hall, *Hall's Illustrated Dictionary of Symbols in Eastern and Western Art*, John Murray (Publishers) Ltd., London, 1994.

John R. Hinells (ed.), *The Penguin Dictionary of Religions*, Penguin Books Ltd., Harmondworth, 1984.

Jessica Hodge, *Who's Who in Classical Mythology*, Bison

Books Ltd., London, 1995.

Nadia Julien, *The Mammoth Dictionary of Symbols: Understanding the Hidden Language of Symbols*, Robinson Publishing, London, 1996.

Jan Knappert, *Pacific Mythology: An Encyclopedia of Myth and Legend*, Diamond Books, London, 1995.

John Laing and David Wire, *The Encyclopedia of Signs and Symbols*, Studio Editions Ltd., London, 1993.

Bernard Lewis (ed.), *The World of Islam: Faith, People, Culture*, Thames & Hudson Ltd., London, 1994.

Carl G. Liungman, *Dictionary of Symbols*, W. W. Norton & Company, New York, 1994.

Mary Miller and Karl Taube, *The Gods and Symbols of Ancient Mexico and the Maya: An Illustrated Dictionary of Mesoamerican Religion*, Thames & Hudson Ltd., London, 1993.

Alexander S. Murray, *Who's Who in Mythology: Classic Guide to the Ancient World*, Bracken Books, London, 1994.

Geoffrey Parrinder, *African Mythology*, Chancellor Press, London, 1996.

Alistair Shearer, *Buddha: The Intelligent Heart*, Thames & Hudson Ltd., London, 1992.

Alan Unterman, *Dictionary of Jewish Lore and Legend*, Thames & Hudson Ltd., London, 1991.

Barbara G. Walker, *The Woman's Dictionary of Symbols and Sacred Objects*, Pandora, London, 1995.

Derek Walters, *Chinese Mythology: An Encyclopedia of Myth and Legend*, Diamond Books, London, 1995.

ACKNOWLEDGEMENTS

The publisher would like to thank Keith Hunt, for illustrations; Lisa Langone Desautels, for the index; Bennett Lovett-Graff of UAHC Press for editorial consultation; and the individuals and institutions listed below, for permission to reproduce photographs on the following pages:
AKG, London: 54tl, 106; Bibliothèque Nationale de Paris: 35; Corbis-Bettmann: 16t, 30t, 43, 52t, 54b, 56t, 62t; CorelDraw: 8t, 9, 10, 12, 17t, 38–39, 40–41, 42b, 44b, 47, 48b, 50b, 51t, 53t, 54tr, 59, 64tr & br, 65tl, 69, 70t, 71bl, 72t, 74, 75, 77b, 79, 82t, 87, 94bl, 95bl, 98tr, 103br & bl, 104t, 107t; FPG International: 16b (© Scott Markewitz 1994), 18t (© Lee Kuhn 1993), 26 (© Mark Scott 1993), 27 (© Carl Roessler 1989), 45t (© Navaswan 1993), 55b (© Ron Thomas 1991), 73b (© Travelpix 1994), 90b (© Dick Luria 1994); Historic Scotland, Ancient Monuments Division: 57; Hulton Deutsch Collection/Corbis-Bettmann: 23b; Library of Congress, Prints and Photographs Division: 33, 34, 90t, 92b; National Archives: 28r; National Archives of Canada: 31b; Planet Art: 7, 8b, 13, 15, 18b, 19t, 20b, 21b, 23t, 29, 31t, 37, 49, 50t, 51b, 53b, 61, 62b, 64l, 70b, 71br, 73t, 76b, 77t, 85, 86, 88, 89, 94t &br, 95t & bl, 96, 97, 98tl & br, 99b, 100t, 101, 102, 103t, 105, 109t; © David Rago: 80b; Saraband Image Library: 36, 71t, 80t, 82b, 83; © Michael A. Smith: 76t; The Southwest Museum, Los Angeles: 32t (HCT 518 MCC.288); UPI/Corbis-Bettmann: 20t, 21t, 22; © Jack Vartoogian: 17b, 63, 67, 72b, 107b; Wyoming State Museum—Division of Cultural Resources: 30b; © Charles J. Ziga: 6, 11, 14, 19b, 24, 25t, 28l, 32b, 46t, 60, 65tr & b, 66, 78, 81, 84, 93, 98bl, 99t, 100b, 108t. Illustrations © **1998**, Keith Hunt.